GW01048792

How to Buy Property in Spain

The Tips and Tricks You Must Know Before You Consider Purchasing Real Estate in Spain

Confessions of a Real Estate Agent

Ian J. Comaskey

Second Edition 2021

Please Read First

Thank you for purchasing "How to buy Property in Spain".
If you follow the tips and tricks continued in the book, you
will save yourself time, stress and cash (more on that later).
You will get the maximum benefit from the book if you
also download the audiobook.
It's 100% free!

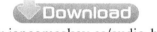

www.iancomaskey.es/audio-book

DEDICATION

This book is dedicated to my co-pilots on this adventure, my crew, my team members!

You people have had to put up with some serious highs, and even more serious lows, since this all began in 2002.

Without any exaggeration, I could not have done this without you. Your hard work and dedication got us here and your humour and friendship kept me going all these years.

Thanks for sticking with me, thanks for everything.

Now, go back to work!!

TABLE OF CONTENTS

ACKNOWLEDGMENTS

First mention is for my wife Lynne who put up with my wild mood swings, coffee highs and late nights of clicking typing sounds, while writing this book.- Thanks. xx

I must acknowledge the encouragement of Amanda Thomas who read, edited, deleted, spelled, proofed and endured the first painful draft of this book.

Sam Adodra from http://www.SeoForBusiness.com for his marketing expertise, Lise and all on the BSBS system - thanks for providing the shoulder to cry on.

Paul Cullen for his sultry tones on the Audiobook version, cheers Paul!

My parents were the ones who introduced me and so many of us to La Zenia in the first place back in 1999. Thanks folks!

My dad Bernie is actually the author in the family so I guess without him, I probably couldn't write. Blame him for this!!

Spanish Solutions who gave me the legal and tax information for the appendix. You guys really know your stuff.

Finally, and most vitally, my clients and non client friends here in Spain. I appreciate your support and all the nice things you say about us. (Even when you don't have to!!)

INTRODUCTION

And we're back…..

Wow, that has been quite an interesting few years since this book first came out. We've successfully(ish) navigated not just Brexit, but also a worldwide pandemic and all the chaos both have brought to the Spanish property market. More about that shortly.

I originally wrote this book in 2014 and we received some wonderful success stories from readers who did, as I suggested, save time, money and stress. I asked when I wrote the book in 2014 that people give us loads of feedback. They did, and it was mostly positive.

Five or six readers (I thought it would be more) came back to me saying that the negotiation tactic saved them at least 5,000 euros each! Result!

It wasn't all positive. I promise these are real comments I received on Facebook;

"The only thing worse than your negotiation technique is your grammar". John.

"The lack of concrete tax information suggests to me that the author does not understand tax in Spain and is making this up as he went along. This is an ad for the author's law firm as he tries unsuccessfully to show us how smart he is". David B.

"Too long" Graham. "Too short" Jane

We helped readers to move to Spain and two readers opened real estate businesses here in order to fund their new life. Another Result!

We assisted many, many more clients with legal and tax issues.

To give Dave B. from the Facebook comments page credit, the point on the lack of tax information was valid. Maybe his delivery was not perfect, but I did ask for feedback.

He is right in that I should have gone into more detail there. I've fixed it for this edition as best I could. It wasn't because I didn't understand the tax laws that I didn't write about them originally. The reality is the rules vary in every region and have changed probably ten times since I wrote this book 7 years ago. The new tax chapter is up top date for the end of 2021 in the Valencia region.

I can't help the fact that we own a law and taxation office and far from being an advertisement for Spanish Solutions, we do offer free advice for those who bought the book but are struggling. Just contact us if you are in doubt; it's free!!

Another point brought up by readers who didn't like the book were regarding my assessment that property purchases in Spain go wrong because of two people.

1. The agent

2. The buyer.

I stand by this. If we could get the bad agents out of the market and get buyers to look at their purchases in a less emotional, more transactional frame of mind, they will save thousands. (you know I'm not exaggerating when I say clients overspend by thousands, this is quite literal).

People said a "buying assistant" makes no sense and I got a few complaints regarding that plan.

"How can someone who does not know me, find the house they know suits me best" Asked Nora on Facebook. It was an easy reply and she ultimately became our client.

"We know the best areas for your most important must-haves and the areas to avoid for your must-not-haves. We know what your budget will buy. You only pay us if we find you a property. With as few as 6 questions, we can tell you what you should and probably will buy, when you come to visit us".

It still works. Since then, half a dozen businesses just offering the service have popped up on the Costa Blanca and the Costa Del Sol. It works. You give your assistant your list; must-haves, must-not-haves and she simply goes to work for you. Again, a good one will save you from 5,000 euro up to 25,000 euro. No joke!

People said that my chapter on the Spanish economy was way out of date. Well, thanks to the aforementioned chaos in the world since March 2020, most of the bad news is being recycled. I think 2022 will be the biggest year on record for foreigners buying property in Spain (if we can find some more to sell!). If I'm right, I'll re-do that chapter next year!

So what about the Spanish property sector itself?

You all know about Brexit, and there is no need to even comment on it. Since 2014 the rules have changed on Non-Europeans (including British people) moving to Spain. In Spanish Solutions, we are helping our British clients with visas and residency and also of course telling them how NOT to buy their property in Spain.

Tips include; Dont buy from anyone who pretends to be me!!

The numbers of property buyers in Spain, (although still unofficial) look to be very good.

There were over 100,000 foreign buyers in Spain in 2017, '18 and '19. 2020 as we know, was a disaster. We look like we'll top 100,000 buyers again in 2021. We'll have stats by Spring 2022 but we're confident of some very strong sales numbers. We know already that we hit 47,500 sales for the first half of 2022 so should top that 100k mark again by the end of the year.

The average spend by the foreigner is increasing too. It was just below 1,800 euro / m2 and prices are increasing.

There is less new build property due to a combination of issues: the Spanish banks, the increasing costs of building materials and labour and naturally as demand is high, developers are taking advantage.

Resales are much more scarce than they were pre-Covid. It is all set up for buyers to make a lot of expensive mistakes unless they really are careful. The buyers are different now too and in many cases younger. Rather than wait until they are at full retirement age, many ex-pats are relocating as they finished their last few years of working life remotely from the comfort of their home in Spain.

There is definitely a large number of "let's just do it now", buyers. They were thinking of owning property here for years and now, after the debacle that was the last year and a half or so, they've decided to do it now.

Most of them will be fine if they employ a good law office first. Yes, John D. from the Facebook comments, I am promoting my own business again!! It's true though, with good legal advice you're 50% less likely to make an expensive mistake.

In other news, I'm now, finally and officially, a retired Spanish estate agent. I sold my company, Comaskey Properties in 2018 with 365,000,000 euro worth of sales completed.

In the years since I've opened an Equity Release company with some terrific people. (JJC CAPITAL Partners). We are now providing liquidity to ex-pat clients who are struggling financially. www.jjccapitalpartners.com

In Spanish Solutions, we've reimagined the law and taxation business. We love to be told something is impossible. We enjoy being the first law firm in Spain to offer "No Win no Fee" options to our clients. We won class actions in the Spanish supreme courts against some of the biggest banks in Spain on behalf of our clients. It has gone really well and we're helping more and more people every day.

Unfortunately, the sale of my company didn't go so well. I can now write the book on how NOT to sell your company in Spain. I made a mistake. I had suspicions about the buyers and chose to ignore them. Worse still, in order to finally get out, I allowed the buyers particularly good terms. I was ready to start my new business so I made a square peg fit into a round hole in my head. The nice people who were supposed to buy us are currently; trading in my name, in my office, with my leads, battering our hard-won reputation and they have paid me less than half of the agreed amount!!

We're taking them to court and they already admitted in writing that they are in a complete breach of contract. This makes the court appearance a formality but bad news for them and their clients.

We have the business back in my name in 2022 and it looks like I'll be moving back into the world of Spanish Real estate. Really, I'm lucky that I have a few wonderful ex Comaskey Properties staff who will run it for me and follow the principles we used for so many years.

So, on to the book itself. Apologies in advance for the spelling/grammar/the book being too long/short and other issues. If you really want to buy a property in Spain and avoid the mistakes that thousands will make in 2022, you'll find the methods in the pages that follow.

Perhaps you need more help? I'm available anytime to chat online with a bit of notice. Even after 3,500 deals completed by Comaskey properties (the real one, NOT the people pretending to be me), I can still help you to make your good decisions better!

If you like the book or if you need any particular help on planning, projecting, writing your lists etc. please do let us know.

Happy house hunting and enjoy your new life in Spain!

(you deserve it!)

Ian Comaskey, Cabo Roig, December 2021.

Buying property in Spain should be simple but not necessarily easy! How often have you assumed you knew how to do something (or could figure it out) because it was simple, only to make a basic error you didn't see coming and didn't know how to avoid? The very simplicity of the task became your enemy, ultimately costing you time, money, and peace of mind.

Did you know the majority of people coming to Spain to buy property end up buying a house they didn't want— before they even started looking at houses? That's right, most buyers go home with the keys to the **wrong house** without even realising it until it's too late. Why? Because they assumed the process was simple, didn't bother to educate themselves about it, made mistakes they may not have even known they were making, and ended up unhappy and trapped.

Do you want to be one of those buyers?

Of course you don't!

Fortunately, you've come to the right place to avoid that fate. This book will explore the mistakes these unfortunate people make every day when buying property in Spain. It will examine why they make these mistakes, how you can avoid them, and how to profit when others continue to make them after you've stopped!

We'll talk about which shortcuts are okay to take and which will trip you up, how to get from the starting point to the perfect property for you with zero stress, the few small actions to take that will put you ahead of 90% of other potential buyers, and how to save thousands of euro and hundreds of hours in the process.

We'll address how to answer the really important questions, like:

- Am I paying too much for my new Spanish home?

- How do I find the best deal in this market?

- How many houses do I need to look at to find the right one?

- Does my real estate agent have my best interests at heart? If not, how can I protect myself, and how can I find one who will?

- Does my real estate agent really know what he's doing? If not, how can I tell?

- Will this agent even still be in business in time to complete the sale?

- Is the house advert accurate? What do I do if it isn't? What happens when the nature reserve the seller told me about across the street looks more like a nuclear power plant?

- Am I being taken advantage of because I'm not a native Spaniard or don't speak Spanish well?

- Spain's economy's been in real trouble recently. How does that impact my potential property purchase?

- How am I supposed to negotiate?

- I'm already paying a lot for this house; will my heirs have to pay a lot more in inheritance taxes to keep it?

- Can't this process just work out so I can enjoy living in Spain already?

We'll show you the biggest mistakes clients have been making since 1999, and how we fixed them for ourselves in our real estate practice. We've sold over 200 million Euros worth of real estate in Spain in the last twelve years, so trust me, we've made plenty of mistakes to learn from! Now we're going to show you how not to repeat them.

"Good advice is priceless. Not what you want to hear, but what you need to hear. Not imaginary, but practical. Not based on fear, but on possibility. Not designed to make you feel better, designed to make you better." ~ **Seth Godin**, *author of "Unleashing the Idea Virus."*

This book will also bring you face to face with your own foibles. Do you know what the superiority trap is? It's one of six psychological flaws humanity falls prey to every time they go to buy anything! We'll show you how you're probably falling into all six traps without even realising, and how to get out of them and stay out.

Do you know how to negotiate? Many people say they do, but studies have shown that only a few actually do. That means most of those people are losing money! Negotiation is not a level playing field, but we'll show you how to make sure everyone wins—especially you! We'll also teach you how to cultivate a calm demeanour under pressure, so you can sit in stressful situations like negotiations without panicking, much like a professional poker player does every day.

And that's just the beginning.

This book will also teach you:

- How to do most of the important work before you come to Spain.

- How to get an estate agent 100% on your side, and for a much lower commission than you might think.

- How our brains are our worst enemies when buying property, and how to beat them.

- What to do when something goes wrong, and how to defeat the negative emotions that accompany these setbacks

- Five absolute must-do tasks that will make the property purchase process absolutely seamless.

- How to not only save thousands of euro on your purchase, but potentially earn thousands in the future through the insider secrets and strategies we employ in our own real estate practice.

If you're ready to find the property of your dreams in Spain, create a simple and foolproof plan for buying it, and glide through the purchase process without breaking a sweat, this book is for you.

Let the fun begin!

Ian Comaskey

October 2014

P.S. This book comes with a money back guarantee. We will gladly refund your money if you do not save a minimum of **3,000 euro** by following our easy system, or you are dissatisfied with this book and our processes for any reason. Give our system a try, and if it doesn't absolutely wow you, we'll pay you back in full.

P.P.S. Leonardo Da Vinci said, "Simplicity is the ultimate sophistication." Yes, this simple system works. Let us show you how. See you on the next page!

Chapter One:
Found Money

In this chapter:

- I will explain that saving money is the very same as finding money. You can find thousands in Spain, maybe tens of thousands by simply buying smart.

Picture yourself walking down a busy main street in any capital city. Think Times Square in New York City or the Champs Elysees in Paris. As you wade through the thousands of people in all directions, you notice a ten-euro bill just lying there right on the ground in front of you, clearly without an owner in sight. What do you do?

If you are the same as 97% of the population, you pick it up and, with the task of finding the owner clearly impossible, you stick it in your back pocket.

Regardless of your personal financial status, nothing feels as good as found money. The world is your oyster, cash for free. You may treat yourself to a Chai Caramel Vanilla Hazelnut white mocha cookie crumble Frappuccino with your bounty or you may stick it in your church poor box. Either way, nothing feels quite like found money.

Now, your day is about to get better. When you actually bend down to pick up what you think is a ten-euro note, you realise that tucked inside the outer layer is a 500-euro note. Suddenly the found money isn't just good, it's fantastic! This is the best day you've had in months. You'll probably tell all your friends about your amazing find.

So now let me ask you a question:

If found money feels this good, why are we so willing to throw away the cash we already have in our pockets?

It's the same thing at the end of the day. The difference between buying the right property in Spain and buying the wrong property in Spain is like the difference between finding 500 euros on the street and dropping 500 euros on the street. Except if you buy the right property in Spain according to the lessons of this book, you won't just save 500 euros. You'll save a lot more.

Think of all the 500-euro notes you could find on the ground inside your bank account. You already had them, but you didn't know they were there until you found them. This is what this book will do for you: uncover all the money you can find by following a few simple rules and practices.

Chapter recap:

- Saved money is found money.

- Found money feels great.

Chapter Two:
But is the Spanish Market terrible?

In this chapter:

- I will explain that the Real Estate market here is one of the best in Europe, especially along the Coast.

There are lots of newspapers these days that love to talk about how it's a terrible time to buy real estate in Spain. The market is down, the market is bad, the market is horrible, it's the worst time to buy, don't even bother, and so forth.

Is that true?

Let's look at a few statistics from the friendly people at the "Ministerio de Fomento" (Spain's Office of Public Works).

In 2013 the total number of completed real estate sales in Spain was 300,568 with a total sales value of 38,075,669,000 Euro.

In terms of regions, here are a few examples of numbers of completions and actual euro values for 2013.

Madrid, the capital: 39,500 deals/ 6,532,113,000 Euro

Murcia, the golf bargain region: 10,000 deals/ 985,500,000 euro

Valencia region, all the way to our office in La Zenia: 48,500 deals/5,610,000,000 Euro

Andalucia, comprising of Almeria, Malaga, Sevilla, Granada: 58,000 deals/7,000,000,000 euro.

Commission paid to estate agents, brokers, banks, under the table bung takers and everyone in between in Spain in 2013 was approximately 1,800,000,000 Euro.

This market is hot! Okay, it's not the really, crazy boom years like in 2008 when the total number of deals completed was a massive 563,000. But still lots of sets of keys are changing hands here; make no mistake.

The point is: if you are getting your perspective on Spanish real estate by reading the press in the UK or even in the rest of Europe then you're not getting the full story or even half of it. The market is much better than these papers believe it is.

Here is one more number: 100

100% is the % of people who would have saved money had they followed the foolproof steps and practices in this book that will find them the right property—and save them money.

Chapter recap:

- Here is the proof if any was needed that the property market is hot in Spain.

Chapter Three:
The 80/20 Rule (Pareto's Principle)

In this chapter:

- Who is Vilfredo Pareto and how can he help save you time and stress in your life?

- What are 80% questions?

- Who asks the wrong questions?

Even if you already know about this principle, you may not be aware just how big an impact it has on your life.

In 1897, Italian economist Vilfredo Pareto observed that 80% of the land in Italy was owned by 20% of the people. The more he observed the world around him the more he saw this uneven balance. He noticed that 80% of the peas his garden produced came from 20% of the pods.

He wore 20% of the clothes in his wardrobe, 80% of the time. He communicated with 20% of his friends 80% of the time. He had unearthed a discovery of enormous importance not just in the world of finance and economics but equally in society, health, education and creativity.

Today it is known as the law of the vital few, the 80/20 rule, or simply Pareto's Principle, and it can be seen in the following modern-day phenomena: 80% of the wealth in the world is owned by 20% of the population.

- 80% of a person's wealth comes from 20% of their activities

- 80% of a company's profit comes from 20% of their sales

- 80% of real estate complaints come from 20% of their clients

- 80% of your success in anything will come from 20% of the work you do

Understanding and capitalising on the 80/20 rule has played a major part in the success stories of today's greatest achievers, people like Bill Gates, Sir Richard Branson, David Bowie and Warren Buffett. And it can play a major part in yours.

So let's flip the rule on its head: 20% of the process of buying real estate in Spain will result in 80% of your success.

You just need to get your 20% right. And getting your 20% right lies in asking the right questions.

Most people in Spain do not buy the right house for the right price. As you might have guessed, the vast majority of successful sales in Spain are completed by the best 20% of estate agents. You need to find the right agent, one who is in the top 20% producing the top results. (Conversely, most of the fiascos, the ones you see on the TV programmes about the horrors of buying property in Spain, come from mistakes made by the *worst* 20% of the agents – avoid these people like the black plague.)

20% of people will buy the right property at the right price. They will not waste time asking themselves the wrong questions, like:

- Do I really need a checklist?

- Can I save money not using a lawyer?

- Are all agents not the same?

- Why should I not borrow a little more than I can afford so I can get that property with the pool?

Instead they will ask 80% success questions:

- Is my agent in the top 20% of sellers in Spain?

- Am I getting the best deal I can?

- Do I trust my agent?

- Is this property ticking all (or 80% at least) of the boxes on my checklist?

Successful investors tend to have a list that contains these tasks:

To do list Success list

Could do Must do

Could do Must do

Must do Must do

Could do

Must do

Could do

Could do

Could do

The to do list is longer, but the success list contains the *vital* few things to be done. Here's how this idea can work for you.

Example of a Spanish property buyer's to do list:

- Contact loads of agents and see who does the best inspection trip

- View loads of houses in different areas

- See if you can get a free meal from your agent

- Look at houses above your price range

- Make sure the furniture is good

- Is the A/C working?

- Make a lot of offers on a lot of houses

- Buy the house where the owner takes the biggest drop in price

- Find out who is the friendliest agent and stick with him

- Pay the deposit in cash

Example of that same buyer's success list:

- Pick the right area

- Get the right agent

- Narrow the search before you get on a plane

- View three houses

- Make an offer, repeat if necessary

- Tidy up the loose ends with your lawyer

The first list contains mostly things that may seem helpful but are secondary to getting the right house. The second list contains only the most essential tasks.

The 80% vs. the 20%.

Chapter recap:

- 80/20 people are starting to dominate business, including real estate, by concentrating on the vital few aspects of the process and forgetting the rest.

- People who wish to benefit from the 80/20 rule can do so by taking some very straightforward steps.

- The top 20% of producers in any peer group is 16 times more effective than the other 80%.

- If an activity has a low return to you either in business or in life, don't do it.

- The law of the vital few is perhaps the most important concept of the past 100 years.

Chapter Four:
Is Buying a House in Spain Worth It?

In this chapter:

- Four ways to benefit from owning a property in Spain. (Apart from a lifetime of memories)

  1. Rental return

  2. Capital Appreciation

  3. Home Exchange

  4. The Golden Visa

If you're moving to Spain permanently, buying a house there is clearly a solid investment. But if you're buying a second home or a vacation property, you may be wondering why a house in Spain is such a great idea. Here are four ways you will profit from your lovely new Spanish house —other than the pleasure of living in it.

1. Rent

When you are not living in the house, you can rent it to tourists, people coming to look for houses to buy, and better still, long term renters who live here all year. Renting is a great way to pocket some extra money from your house. If you're savvy enough, you can even cover your own mortgage payments on the house by renting it out.

Technically there are two ways to rent out your house: do it yourself, or find a rental company to do it for you. But since you may be living in a completely different country while renting out your house in Spain, only one of those options truly makes sense. If you live abroad and manage your property yourself it will end in tears. It won't work.

On the other hand a good property management company will:

- vet the tenants, refusing those who will cause you trouble down the road;

- complete the paperwork, (direct debits, contracts, utilities etc);

- fill in an inventory;

- ensure you are getting paid;

- keep you up to date as to how it's working out with your tenants;

- deal with immediate tenant needs such as repairs, loss of keys, that sort of thing.

How do you find a good rental company?

I saw this ad recently for a rental company in Spain. I did not make this up. This is their ad, I changed the name to Acme Rentals.

We charge NO commission. (Uh, oh, already I'm worried, how are these guys going to make money!)

Renters book direct with owners, no letting agents involved *(why would I not want letting agents??)*

Free link to your own website and telephone number. (What? The potential client contacts me... In Denmark) Spanish leases with English translation prepared. (Great, thanks, that's important, what about other languages though?)

A quarter of a million visitors to the site p.a. (That's good, but there is more rental demand than supply so filling the property won't be an issue, I want the right tenant)

Cost to advertise for 12 months just £80 or 100 Euros. (Now we get an idea of what's going on, you pay them up front then YOU do the work.)

People looking to rent in Spain up-to 2 years in advance. (Seriously, I'm not making this up. these guys want you to sign an agreement to rent your house in two years from now??)

Practical, friendly bi-lingual advice to help let your house. *(Bi-lingual? What about German, French, Swedish....)*

This will be a disaster for anyone who uses this service. The problem starts when they tell me they charge "no commission." Run away from this sort of company, fast!

Here are a few points on finding a quality rental company:

Get an agent

- Make sure they know what they are doing, ask who prepares the contract, is it legally binding?

- Does your agent vet the tenants? How? Do they ask for work contracts, bank statements etc?

- Can they provide testimonials?

- Do they handle property management?

- And the least important question (within reason) what percentage do they charge? 12-15% is about right here in Spain.

When buying, make sure you buy in the right rental area. Renters, like buyers, 80% of the time want to be within walking distance to the sea, to the shops, bars and restaurants and possibly the medical centre.

Please be aware:

You'll probably earn less than you think renting your house, any house, anywhere.

My rental department will *love* me for saying this. It's easy to anticipate the rent coming in and forget that you are liable for tax on the money. Then there are upkeep and repair costs: outside wall needs painting, the washing machine needs replacing, and the community fee needs to be paid.

Make sure to plan for all of these costs, get yourself a decent rental agency, and pay your tax on time to avoid nasty surprises and fines.

The most important part of renting your house is buying right in the first place.

Just so you don't think I get it right all the time, here is my story of renting in Ireland from 2001 for ten years or so.

I decided to rent my house privately – apart from the fact I absolutely needed the money, I figured, I'm pretty smart (superiority trap). I lived 2,000 KM away. That's not a good thing and my tenants were very aware of that fact.

This was pre-internet banking so I did not know if the rent was being paid. Worse still, I didn't call the bank every month to check it. This was just pure procrastination as I didn't want to receive bad news about the rent not going into my account.

Often the clients part paid, telling me they had to replace a washing machine or something – I never looked for receipts.

I did not inspect the property and had no signed inventory.

In all those years, I never had a tenant who paid the full amount and most of them left the house in a worse state than when they moved in.

My last tenants caused 20,000 euro worth of damage. Every door was broken (like they had been kicked in) and the ceiling in the kitchen collapsed due to a tap that was left running in the bathroom overhead.

The house stank of smoke including the main bedroom.

Mirrors, the bath, the boiler, the aluminum back door, beds, mattresses, the flower beds, my TV and other appliances, all ruined and all my own fault for not doing the job properly and hiring a property management company.

2. Sell for a higher price

The second way to profit from your purchase in Spain is appreciation.

I used to tell our buyers that you could buy a shed in a field in 2006 and flip it for a massive profit within two weeks. Back in the day we meant it when we told people their investment would appreciate massively in a short term. The average appreciation in 2007 in Spain was **30%**!

Can these days ever return? Well, they can, but not for a while. The market is picking up but this sort of massive appreciation is a bit of a way off in the future.

Once you buy at the lowest price possible <u>in the best area</u> you can make money on property price appreciation in the medium term.

An example of how to profit from "flipping" in 2014 is the following:

A seller, call him George, has a house worth 110,000 euro (this figure is based on the selling prices around him within the past few months). He was trying to sell privately rather than employ an agent so he didn't get any genuine offer and now is in financial trouble.

He owes the bank 90,000 and is struggling to meet the re-payments, in fact he is about to have the house repossessed, costing him even more in legal fees and potentially damaging his credit rating.

Because he is three months behind in his mortgage payments potential buyers are put off that there may be more complications and the house may be repossessed before completion even takes place. Also the condition of the house is poor as he rented it privately to non-paying tenants who did not take care of the property.

This may not seem like a great property. But really it's the dream for the property flipper because you can help everyone.

Offer George 90,000 cash to clear the debt and take on all expenses from that point forward. As a sweetener for him, offer to cover George's solicitor fees up to 1,000 euro. Happy George, no more headache.

Through your agent, you pay a deposit of 6,000 euro to the bank if they agree to pay George's outstanding debts (community fees, electricity, water bills, local taxes etc.). They will be happy as it saves them going to court to get the property in their name. This can save them up to two years of legal wrangling while the condition of the property worsens all the time. Note, they will clear all of George's outstanding debts. Happy bank, one less repo on their books.

Get your agent to recommend someone who can stage your house – get it painted, give it a serious clean and leave it ready to view. 2,000 euro budget. Happy house.

Now sell it for 105,000 euro to a happy client agreeing to pay your agent a reasonable commission. The agent will reduce their fees if you are fair to them and if you suggest this will be a regular type of deal that you do. Happy agent.

Investment:

- George's legal fees 1,000

- Your legal fees 1,000

- Deposit, (which the new buyer refunds to you) 6,000

- Staging the house 2,000

- Reduced commission to the agent to find you a buyer 4,000

You don't pay any purchase tax or notary fees as you never own the house.

Total outlay - 14,000. Total profit after expenses - 7,000 Euro. Happy Buyer.

Not bad and when you get good at this you can look at other strategies including getting finance for your buyer through the bank holding the mortgage, thus making it even easier to get a buyer.

However as a word of warning: if you can't get a buyer, if your agent or solicitor is not experienced in this kind of thing, you could be stuck with the house or even lose your deposit on the property.

Just be careful!

In reality, old fashioned property appreciation in Spain is still a reason why so many investors are buying here. It would be unfair of me to promise you that if you buy now the property will appreciate 100% in five years. It might, but it's not the job of an estate agent to tell you that. We have seen property prices drop 40, 50 and even 60% in some cases during the property market collapse. That means surely the price has got to increase once buyers regain confidence in late 2014 and 2015. I believe this and I'm betting my money on it but you must do your own due diligence. One thing for sure if you want to see appreciation on your purchase in Spain: you must buy the right house at the best possible price – then you are giving yourself a real chance of success.

3. Home exchange

I'm writing this part in Paris, France in the summer of 2014. We are staying in a stranger's home. My sister is here with her kids, our two boys are playing in the garden and my parents arrive in tonight.

We have joined "HomeExchange.com" and we are on our fourth exchange.

The general idea is that we come and stay in someone else's house and they stay in ours. We exchange keys and cars in the airport and quite literally we have the full run of their house while they have the same in ours.

You know the funny thing when you own a house in Spain within walking distance of the sea? You'll get requests for the most amazing locations and houses in the world – no exaggeration.

For us, because we live in Spain all year round, August is a great time to get out – the complete opposite direction to the way most people are travelling.

This is not a money saver as such—but it's a serious stress saver. We get a car, (actually two cars as it turned out), baby stuff, golf equipment, free WIFI and a computer, TV – and when you travel like this you see far more of where you go as opposed to staying in a hotel.

We use HomeExchange.com but there are loads of sites to choose from with a selection of about 50,000 homes everywhere in the world. We were recently offered exchanges in Costa Rica and New Zealand and we swapped with a couple in Toronto last summer.

This system is particularly suited to anyone who owns a *second* home in Spain. Try it and you'll be amazed. I totally recommend it.

Exchanges do not have to be simultaneous. You can fly from your home in Sweden to Toronto for a week and your exchangers from Toronto will travel to your apartment on the golf course in Spain for two weeks if that is what you agree.

You never meet but you've spoken plenty by email and phone in order to vet each other. We have not heard of any cases where the exchange went wrong.

If you want more info on how it works just send me an email.

4. Golden Visa

European Investment visas were introduced by the EU a couple of years back to specifically attract wealthy non EU nationals to Europe or more precisely to allow rich people earn European citizenship.

- Spain, France, UK, Portugal, Cyprus and Ireland introduced an option called the "golden visa."

Here's how it works:

If a non-European invests 500,000 (plus VAT) in Spain right now, we can all but guarantee them a golden visa. Those holding a golden visa are allowed to travel to any of the 26 countries and principalities within the Schengen area, including the Vatican!

Each country has different and varied regulations, none of them easy, yet Spain appears to be one of the most willing to accept new residents.

The requirements for this investment are as follows:

- The money must be cash – i.e. the client cannot get a mortgage for 450,000 and only invest 50,000 of their own money.

- The money can be mortgaged from investments or home equity outside Europe.

- The investment can be in either a business or residential property. It can also be a combination of both.

- The visa is valid for not just the main investor but for his/her immediate family also.

- You cannot have a criminal record or be a terrorist.

- The vast majority of investments and purchases in Spain are valid. Make sure that the property or business is in the scheme before you purchase it. Check with a lawyer and make sure your agent is aware why you are buying.

- There is no official minimum amount of time successful candidates must remain in the country.

- If all the paperwork is correct and your investment is valid, the visa can be obtained within 15 working days!

Important to know: There is another type of visa available in Spain with no minimum investment involved. Applicants must be prepared to spend 6 months per year here.

It means non-residents can effectively avail of the benefits of the golden visa, with residential investments of 100,000 euro for example.

There are now cheap direct flights from Spain available to Asia, Russia and the Middle East in the hope of attracting families to live here half of the year at least and commute back home for the rest of the time.

Chapter recap:

- There are more ways to benefit from owning a home in Spain apart from enjoying 320 days of sunshine.

Chapter Five:
Special Notes for American, Russian and Chinese Buyers

Please note: This chapter is not about singling out countries for any kind of racism or nationalism. Unfortunately buyers from these countries tend to run into rather unique issues when buying property in Spain, and I'd feel remiss if I didn't address those issues here. If you are not from these countries but not from Spain either, feel free to read on as well.

A Russian gentleman said this to me a few months ago at a property exhibition in Moscow: "I like you and have learned a lot from you." I thought this was going well, having spent half an hour together telling him the best areas, the prices, costs, golden visa details, etc.

Then he said that he won't buy from us because he is used to a higher level of luxury inspection trip than what I told him we normally do, and because he was afraid we'd try too hard to sell him something. Suddenly anything else I had to say seemed like trying too hard. The more I tried to convince him that we were not a typical sales company, the more I sounded like a desperate salesman.

He didn't buy from us and I don't know how much he spent in the end. It's a shame because he had a real chance of working with a quality agent and passed it up.

Three relatively new streams of property buyers in Spain are buyers from Russia, China and the U.S. 20% of property purchasing in Spain is from non-nationals, with these three nationalities alone making up 30% of that investment.

We recently attended property exhibitions in Beijing and Moscow to try and find out from the people on the ground what they really want in property and what they expect from their agent. As far as I can see you want to be able to trust the agent, to be treated luxuriously, and to make your own decisions rather than be pitched and sold to.

The problem then becomes a cultural thing. Irish and English agents (there are many of us in Spain) like to do the sale in a more efficient manner. We as a general rule are more concerned in getting the best price possible and pay less attention to the personal side of the sale. We don't take our clients for lunch, or drive them around in air-conditioned Hummers. We just don't think like that. Foreign buyers sometimes see this as a lack of service and this is not our intention. Without sounding cold, we just want to get the deal closed and move onto the next client.

Therefore Russian and Chinese clients often seek out and buy from agents from their own countries who will treat them in the way they want and expect to be treated. That in itself is not an issue, but problems can occur when in some cases those agents are not capable of negotiating with the sellers as well as English or Irish agents would be.

Remember that the seller is unlikely to be from your country so you are totally alien to them. Also they probably are not business people, just property owners. You might as well be from Mars as from Moscow.

The person cutting the deal (your agent) has got to have experience dealing with Irish, English and Spanish sellers.

Ironically, for the agent to have a knowledge of your country and systems is not that important, since the sale is not taking place in your country.

Another problem that comes up for foreign buyers: when the seller knows the buyer is Russian or Chinese, the price goes up. I have seen sellers absolutely refuse to drop their price to American, Russian and Chinese buyers *and agents* simply because they know they are American, Russian and Chinese.

These sellers assume you will pay more. Many Spanish sellers have anchored to the (incorrect) idea that Americans, Russians and Chinese spend money frivolously. So they charge you more.

What you have got to do is agree a fee with the agent in advance, or better still find a buying assistant who will process the deal for you on a flat fee basis. Sign a tight contract with them and they are suddenly on your side trying to get the best deal for you. This would save you millions of euro in commissions and it would mean you are much less likely to pay too much for your property purchase.

A buying assistant with a good legal translator will cost you 5,000 per week and will agree to process your sale for zero commission. You'll have no stress, no sales pitch and will save a small fortune.

Imagine if instead of paying up to 15% commission you hired a sales assistant and a translator with the following qualities:

- They are professional

- They can deal with <u>sellers</u> from different countries. This is more important than knowledge of the system in China or Russia

- They can demonstrate that they can obtain visas for their buyers. The process of obtaining visas is complex and must be done absolutely correctly

- They will send brochures to the buyer before they even leave for the airport which will match the buyer's check list

- They show these properties listed on a number of websites and property portals so the buyer can see there is no manipulation of the price. (That is, not one price for a Russian buyer but another price for a Spanish buyer.)

- They have at least 100 testimonials

- They speak multiple languages or work with people who do. They can negotiate in Spanish and English

- They are tax compliant (Non negotiable)

- They can write contracts, have an independent lawyer on call, are able to take deposits and close deals

In other words, they can take care of all your real estate needs for you. Find this agent. Contract them to work with you as an assistant, pay them very well before you start your search and you will save a small fortune. I absolutely guarantee it, you need these assistants more than anyone else and way more than you think you do.

Testimonial from happy Chinese client

From: 朱慧芳
Subject: the letter in English
To: Ian Comaskey <ian@comaskey.com>

"Hello Ian!

I will write the content of the letter in Chinese, use English to write you a look, you know my English is not good, may have some place to write English is wrong, please forgive me!

I heard you are writing a book about Spain, I am sincerely admire your talent and happy for you!Remember the first time 13 hours fly long distances to come to Spain ali leftover, your office, SHWAN and ELLENA with H and I went to the beach, near the city, the shops around the shop, I was attracted by the beautiful scenery and quiet life here.H regrets ground say: "life happiness index is not high in here!"

Thank you very much, busy two days, whole SHWANG drive very hard with us in the urban area selected a set of the HOUSE, I am very satisfied.This HOUSE is my dream HOUSE, first of all, it is very beautiful!Three floors of large balcony sunshine, can let my child and I on the sunshine and the number of the stars at night.

The bedroom on the second floor of the room is very vital qi, the two rooms to the south, outside the room has a big balcony, very let me joy!West of a large bedroom with a bathroom and a balcony, feeling will have a good dream my inside!On the first floor of the hall has a very large area, atmosphere and style very much!

Sunny and fireplace, Christmas my daughter and I can read in front of the fireplace and the game!On the first floor there is a toilet, kitchen and one in the workshop.Facilities is full and the work place is very big, I think my housework operation will be very handy!Outside on the first floor hall has a large terrace, terrace is a big garden outside.

Can accommodate more than a dozen friends in the garden and terrace for rest and entertainment!Second, my HOUSE's geographical location and the surrounding environment is I am very satisfied.Beside the HOUSE, walk ten minutes is a very good school, thank ELLENA took us to visit that day, communicate with school teachers of the children learn.

That school has rich experience in teaching, the teachers are very friendly and love!We introduced them to a Spanish citizenship has a wealth of experience in teaching foreign children, because their school children with nine different countries where reading, also asked me about children see also gave me some.

This makes me very relieved and happy!Will have long left their own country and family life with children choose to live in Spain, children can get a good education is one of my mother's biggest wish!In addition, house community environment is very good, my neighbor is British and Spanish.

Look have higher literacy and very friendly manners!Feel and do their neighbors will be very happy.House on a hill, you can also see at a distance coastline, the whole community environment is very beautiful, clean swimming pool and other facilities is also very important!

When I come back to China, I bought the HOUSE photos first experience in Spain and I told my Chinese friends, they are very like my HOUSE, very impressive!I have relatives and friends in Canada, in Australia, in New Zealand, they all know before I go to Spain have been looking for a New Zealand lawyer working on the New Zealand immigration visa formalities, why will change my mind to go to Spain? I told the I chose Spain reason to my friends.

The first and the most important thing is the Spanish is a very important country in Europe, where there are beautiful scenery and pleasant climate.Life for children.Choose Europe because Europe has my child and I have a passion for the long history and culture, my child has a gift for her on the drawing!

This in China, her painting talent to the teacher evaluation is very high, the teacher want us to do the parents to find the opportunity to develop more in this respect.But Europe is a paradise of art.Spain's national in art is also a leader! Children like to dance, I want her to learn Spanish the world-famous paso doble, Flamenco, tango.

The Spanish language is also one of the five major languages in the world, the United States of California Asia, South America is very common in many parts of the world, not only in TORREVIEJA area has beautiful scenery and there are a lot of British people living in this area, I think my children live here and learning, can learn English and Spanish, that is my most happy things.

After I think she can go to try to know more about the world when he grows up.Learn more knowledge, rich experience of her life.To become a useful person can make a little contribution in the world!This is my choice for children living in the main reason of Spain.Second, Spain and China has always been very good, the relationship between the two countries are friends, Spain's prime minister, just to visit China this is known to all, the two countries economic cooperation in the future will be is a good time, I recommend all my friends can go to the Spanish national tourism, introduce them to Spain to see here rich in agricultural products and modern science and technology.

There are a lot of business opportunities can be reference for them! Here I thank you again for IAN and his colleagues in the company to give my help!When I apply for your visa formalities here will happily belt daughter lives to Spain!I look forward to an early to go to Spain in this beautiful and god of country!"

"您好，Ian!

听说您在写一本关于西班牙的书，我真是由衷地敬佩您的才华和替你感到高兴！记得第一次坐飞机十三个小时不远万里地来到西班牙阿里茨特您办公室，SHWAN 和 ELLENA 带着我和 H 去海边，城区附近，商店到处逛了逛，我就被这里美丽景色和安静的生活所吸引。H 感慨地说："生活在这里幸福指数不可能不高！"

非常感谢你们，整整忙了两天，SHWANG 开车很辛苦陪我们在城区里挑选了一套我本人非常满意的 HOUSE。这间 HOUSE 是我梦想中的房子，首先，它非常漂亮！三层楼的阳台很大很阳光，可以让我和孩子在上面晒太阳和夜晚数星星。二楼的卧室房型很正气，朝南面二个房间，房间外有一个大露台，非常让我欢喜！西面的一个大卧室带一个卫生间和一个露台，感觉睡在里面我就一定会做好梦！一楼的大厅面积很大，非常大气和气派！阳光充足且还有壁炉，圣诞节我和女儿可以在壁炉旁看书和游戏！一楼还有个卫生间，厨房间和一个在的工作间。设施很全而且工作地方很大，我想我操作家务会非常得心应手！一楼大厅外还有个很大的露台，露台外面是一个很大的花园。可以容下十多个朋友在花园和露台里休息和娱乐！其次，我的 HOUSE 所处的地理位置和周边的环境是我很满意的。 HOUSE 的旁边走路十几分钟就是一个很好的学校，感谢 ELLENA 那天带我们去学校参观，跟学校的老师交流了下孩子学习的情况。那个学校有丰富的教学经验，老师非常友好和慈爱！给我们介绍了他们对非西班牙国籍的外籍孩子有着丰富的教学经验，因为他们学校有九个不同国家的孩子在那里读书，还问了我孩子的一些情况也给了我一些见议。这使我非常放心和快乐！必竟不远万里离开自己生活的国家和家庭带孩子选择在西班牙生活，孩子能够得到良好的教育是我一个做母亲的最大心愿！另外，房子所处的社区环境很好，我的邻居是英国人和西班牙人。看上去都有着较高的素养和非常友好的礼节！感觉和他们做邻居会很快乐。房子在一个小山坡上，远远地还可以看见海岸线，整个社区环境非常优美，游泳池和其他设施也非常齐全和干净！

当我回到中国，把我买的 HOUSE 照片和我在西班牙的第一次经历告诉我的中国朋友们，他们都非常喜欢我的 HOUSE，非常赞叹！我有亲戚和朋友在加拿大，在澳大利亚，在新西兰，他们都知道在我去西班牙之前都已经找了新西兰的律师在办新西兰的移民签证手续了，为什么会改变我的心意去了西班牙？我把我选择西班牙的理由告诉了我的朋友们。首先也是最重要的一点是西班牙在欧洲是个很重要的国家，这里风景优美，气候宜人。适合孩子生活。选择欧洲是因为欧洲有我孩子和我都酷爱的悠久的历史和文化，我的孩子在画画上有她的天赋！这个在中国，她画画的天赋让她的教师评价很高，老师希望我们做家长的能够找到机会在这方面多培养她。而欧洲可是个艺术的天堂啊。西班牙国家在艺术上也是个佼佼者！孩子喜欢跳舞，我想让她学习西班牙举世闻名的斗牛舞，Flamenco, tango. 另外西班牙的语言也是世界上五大语种之一，美国的加里福利亚洲，南美洲世界上很多地方都很通用，在 TORREVIEJA 地区不仅有美丽的风景而且还有很多英国人住在这个地区，我想我的孩子在这里生活和学习，能够学会英语和西班牙语，那是我最最开心的事情。我想她以后长大了可以去尝试着多了解世界。多学习知识，丰富她的人生经验。成为一个能为世界作出点小小贡献的有用的人！这是我为孩子选择生活在西班牙的最主要的原因。其次，西班牙和中国的关系一直都很好，两个国家是朋友，西班牙首相刚到中国访问过这个大家都知道的，两个国家在以后的经济合作上会是一个很好的时机，我推荐我所有的朋友们都可以到西班牙国家旅游，介绍他们来西班牙看看这里丰富的农产品和现代化科技。有很多的商业机会可以供他们参考！

在这里我再次感谢 IAN 和他的公司里同事们给予我的帮助！等我这里办好签证手续就会高高兴兴地带女儿去西班牙生活！我期待能早日去到西班牙这个美丽和神密的国家！"

Chapter recap:

- If you are Russian, American or Chinese in particular, there are more things that can go wrong when buying property in Europe and especially in Spain.

Chapter Six:
Tax in Spain

"It is every person's obligation to pay the correct amount of tax; not one euro less nor one euro more."

Tony Robbins.

Tax is stressful. Tax in Spain is worse. Anyone who has had any dealings with the Agencia Tributaria (The Spanish tax authorty) will know what we are talkng about.

Here we mention some of the latest rules and regulations. These rules change and I am not a tax advisor. Rafael Hernandez, our Spanish tax expert is available to discuss in more detail with our clients at any time.

Let's start with the Spanish tax rates.

Spain's tax bands currently are the following:

- Up to €12,450: 19%

- €12,450–€20,200: 24%

- €20,200–€35,200: 30%

- €35,200–€60,000: 37%

- €60,000–€300,000: 45%

- more than €300,000: 47%

There have been a few additions to the rules this year.

The tax rate for savings income exceeding €200,000 increased by 3%.

The Spanish Government this year also implemented two new tax reforms. The FTT tax, or financial transaction tax and the DST, digital service tax are new. These reforms are aimed at large corporations and high earners.

The bands are the basic Spanish tax rates on employment income. Tax rates in Spain are not the same across the country and clients total tax liability is confusing. Clients need to use the state's general tax rates plus the relevant regional tax rates to find the accurate amount.

Spanish tax deductions and allowances.

It's not all bad news. Deductions are key to reducing your tax liability in Spain.

All residents in Spain receive certain tax deductions. The personal allowance is the following;

- €5,550 under the age of 65

- €6,700 from age 65,

- €8,100 from age 75.

A resident with children under 25 living at home, you can claim additional allowances:

- €2,400 for the first child.

- €2,700 for the second.

- €4,000 for the third.

- €4,500 for the fourth.

- €2,800 additionally for each child under three years.

Those with a parent or grandparent living at home, with a total income less than €8,000, can claim one of two allowances.

- €1,150 if they are over 65

- €2,550 if they are over 75.

Once they receive correct advice, clients claim tax deductions for: Spanish pension contributions.

Social security system payments in Spain

Expenses associated with buying and renovating your main home charitable donations.

The latest new tax reforms reduced taxpayers' pension contributions for tax purposes to €2,000. Previously it was €8,000. This limit of €8,000 is still valid if the increase comes from company contributions. Any increase cannot exceed 30% of the sum of net income from employment and economic activities received.

Capital gains tax in Spain. (CGT)

Spain's capital gains tax is not crystal clear. Like it is worldwide, CGT in Spain is the tax on profits from selling a property or other investments.

You may be eligible for an exemption if you are over age 65 and selling your main home. People may also be eligible if they are under 65 and selling their main home to buy another main home in Spain. Readers of the blog can see now why we say to our clients, talk to us before you buy or sell your property in Spain! If you bought your Spanish property before 1994, you may be liable to pay more tax than before.

Current the rates are;

- First €6,000, 19%.

- €6,000–€50,000, 21%.

- €50,000–€200,000, 23%.

- more than €200,000, 26%.

Spanish wealth tax

The Wealth tax in Spain is payable on the value of your assets. This year the Spanish government increased the highest tax band rate by 1% in autonomous communities where they have yet to approve their own rates. Assets valued at more than €10 million can be taxed up to 3.5%, depending on the particular region.

There is a €700,000 tax-free allowance. Property owners here are allowed a further €300,000 against the value of their main residence.

Inheritance and gift tax in Spain

This is worthy of a whole blog all to itself. It is currently the tail end of 2021, and as far as we know, everything is about to change.

Previously, non-residents in Spain paid around 80% more than Spanish residents on inheritance tax. The Spanish Supreme court ruled this was illegal. Since then, non-residents who paid the higher rate in the past are entitled to a refund.

In 2017, some regions updated their inheritance and gift tax policies, others did not. Many families found themselves not having to pay inheritance tax at all. Valencia is about to introduce a change and we await to see what it means. Check your specific region's laws with Rafael in Spanish solutions.

The rate is around 1–7% for all, depending on the region.

Tax in Spain for married couples

Married couples can choose to be taxed separately or together. You should compare the Spanish tax rate and speak to Rafa before you decide. There is a married couple's allowance of €3,400 called a declaración conjunta for the second taxpayer. Additionally, there is a general allowance of €5,550 granted to the first taxpayer. This applies to couples either in a heterosexual or same-sex marriage.

Spanish property tax

So many of our clients were told that they did not have to pay tax on their property in Spain by over-eager real estate agents; not true, unfortunately.

Can we say it again; Please talk to us before you buy or sell your property in Spain.

If you sell a property in Spain, you have to pay a property transfer tax, also known as ITP, Impuesto Transmisiones Patrimoniales. Plus Valia is another tax and is charged by the local authority on the increase in the value of the land. If it's an apartment the cost is approximated.

IBI tax is payable if you are living in your Spanish property on 1 January in any given year. It is also called the Impuesto Sobre Bienes Inmuebles (local tax). The amount payable is the rental value of the property times a tax rate set by the local town hall. This tax is due for non-residents and residents.

Property owners may need to pay the basura, a rubbish collection tax. Of course, Spanish property owners may also need to pay income tax at flat rates on potential rental income.

Tax in Spain for non residents.

The income tax rate for non-residents in Spain is 24%. It is 19% if you are a citizen of an EU state. Yes, I know, Brexit. That is why we have a tax expert working with our British clients in Spain!

Spanish non-resident taxes are due at the following rates;

CGT as already mentioned is taxed at a rate of 19%.

Investment interest and dividends are taxed at 19%. These through double taxation agreements are usually less.

Interest tax is ZERO for EU citizens. (finally good news)

Royalties are taxed at 24%.

Your pension will be taxed at progressive rates, from 8% to 40%.

To apply to pay income tax as a non-resident of Spain, you need to get a Modelo 149. The Modelo 150 is where you sign off on your income tax declaration. A Modelo 210 will be required if you are a non-resident property owner in Spain.

Foreigners working on an assignment in Spain.

If you are working on a special contract with a Spanish company, there is a unique tax regime. This is often referred to as Beckham's Law since 2003. It was allegedly set up so that Posh and Becks did not have to pay tax on his worldwide image rights (Gillette and Adidas) when he joined Real Madrid.

You may or may not play for Real Madrid. You'll pay a 24% tax rate on income up to €600,000 if employed on assignment in Spain.

You'll pay 47% however on income in Spain that exceeds €600,000. Temporary relocated employees now pay 3% tax on income above €200,000 that is generated from CGT, dividends or interest.

If you are a Spanish tax resident and have not been resident in Spain in the last 10 years, you can apply to be taxed under this regime. You must do so within six months of arriving in Spain. You can reduce your taxation level for up to five years if you deal with this properly.

Register to pay Spanish tax: residents and non-residents

Spanish solutions of course deal with the tax affairs of thousands of ex-pats living in Spain. Literally thousands.

If you decide to do it yourself, first, you need to register to pay tax in Spain previously mentioned Agencia Tributaria. This is true whether you are a resident or non-resident in Spain. You'll need your NIE or Foreigner's Identity Card, which you can get through the local Foreigner's Office (Known here as the Oficina de Extranjeros). You can apply in your local police station within 30 days of landing in Spain. The Modelo 30 is needed to register your obligation to pay Spanish tax as a resident or non-resident for the first time, or even to change your details. The easiest way to obtain an NIE is through Spanish Solutions.

Tax in Spain; Filing your tax return.

You must file a Spanish tax return in the first year of tax residency. Telling the authorities that you didn't know is not a good defence. (Yes, talk to Spanish Solutions before you move to Spain!!)

After year one, you don't have to file a Spanish tax return if;

- Your income from all sources is less than €8,000

- you have less than €1,600 of bank interest or investment income

- if your rental income is less than €1,000

- you earn less than €22,000 as an employee, as in this case, your employer will have already deducted your Spanish income tax.

- As always please check with a professional before making your declarations or deciding whether or not the rule applies to you.

The tax year in Spain runs in line with the calendar. You must file tax returns between 6 April and 30 June of the following year. There are not any extensions on filing tax returns in Spain.

Even if you choose not to work with Spanish Solutions, we can, hand on heart say managing your tax in Spain will be much easier with the help of an accounting and tax advice professional.

IVA (VAT) in Spain

There are three levels of IVA (Impuesto Sobre el Valor Añadido) in Spain:

21 % General rate on goods and services.

10 % Reducido rate on items such as; exhibitions, health products, non-basic foods, transport, tolls, amateur sporting events, rubbish collection, pest control, wastewater treatment.

4% Superreducido on essential foods, medicine, books, and newspapers.

The government increased IVA from 10% to 21% on alcoholic drinks and drinks containing added natural and derived sweeteners and/or sweetening additives just this year. Excluded from the hike are baby milk and drinks considered as food supplements for special dietary needs.

VAT payers in Spain must submit all invoices online to the tax authority in Spain within four days of the date of issuance; no later than the 16th day of the month following its issue.

Corporate tax rates and rules in Spain

Spain has a general rate of corporate tax of 25%.

New companies pay a reduced 15% for the first two years of business.

A reduction of 10% in tax may be granted to profits locked into a special reserve for 5 years. Spanish SL Companies must file tax returns within six months and 25 days after the end of the accounting period. Payment generally is made in instalments during April, October, and December. These instalments usually are 18% of the tax liability.

Am I a Spanish tax resident or non-resident?

We are asked this all the time.

My account from years past Alex Sanchez used to tell clients;

If you live in Spain, you're a resident.

Alex was trying to say that people should know where they live! The clearer explanation is that;

if you have been living in Spain for 183 days in any year (not necessarily consecutively)

if you have your main vital interests in Spain (your family!)

Or if your business is here in Spain, then you are classed as a Spanish resident for tax purposes.

In this case, you must submit a Spanish tax return.

You pay income tax on your worldwide profits if any of the following is true; your annual income from employment is more than €22,000; you run your own business in Spain; receive rental income of more than €1,000 a year; have capital gains and savings income of more than €1,600 a year or it is your first year declaring tax residency in Spain.

You must declare all your assets abroad worth more than €50,000 (Form 720) every year.

If, on the other hand, as Alex Sanchez would explain, you live in Spain for less than six months (183 days) in a calendar year, you are a non-resident. In this case, you only pay tax on the money you earn in Spain.

Tax is liable on your income at flat rates and no allowances or deductions are permissible. If you own Spanish property, whether or not you rent it out, you will need to submit a tax return. You must also pay Spanish property taxes for non-residents as well as local Spanish property taxes.

Conclusion: Spanish tax is difficult.

Clients of Spanish Solutions are very lucky to have one of the most capable tax advisors at hand in the shape of Rafa Hernandez. You can read more about Rafa on the blog post we dedicated to him.

https://www.spanishsolutions.net/blog/taxes-in-spain/a-new-tax-expert-joins-the-team/

It is possible to go it alone but we strongly recommend that you speak to Rafa before you open your business in Spain and especially if you intend to buy or sell a property in Spain.

We have special deals available to ensure you pay little or nothing to Rafa, once you use Spanish Solutions to take care of your conveyancing.

Why not speak to us first, before you even start searching for an estate agent in Spain?

We can save you many thousands of euros!

enquiries@spanishsolutions.net
0034:966761741

Finally, I'm sorry that even this revised chapter is not crystal clear. You need to speak to an expert, and there are many, despite the fact I constantly tell you how good our man is! Every deal is different, depending on where it is, what the town hall says it's worth, what you are really paying etc. Be careful take your time and get this right.

Chapter Seven:
Location, Location, Location

In this chapter:

- It's not where you buy, it's what you buy.

- How Polaris World Golf Resort *almost* worked.

- A cheap house is generally cheap because that's what someone is willing to pay for it.

If you go online, you can find all kinds of forums and "guide to buying property in Spain" websites. These sites appear to know exactly where you should buy in Spain, and have plenty of recommendations on that topic.

This book is not going to tell you where to buy, because you don't need to know where to buy. This book is going to tell you HOW to buy. Buying property in Spain the right way makes sure that you find the right property for you— and that includes the property's location.

Let's talk about geography for a moment. Most of the recommendations from the "property guide" websites and forums will advise buying in different geographical regions or cities because of the beautiful countryside or the cities' amenities.

Some of them will be very persuasive in selling a particular area. But remember that a good area in general doesn't necessarily mean a good area for you!

This is where your checklist comes in.

Now, you can have a location on your checklist. But instead of thinking about particular cities or areas of the country right away, think about location by category. Some of the different categories you might think of include:

- Beach

- City

- Inland

- Mountains

- Islands

- Golf

- Forest

Once you decide which geographical category you want to live in, then you can narrow down your location requirements from there.

For example, maybe you want to live in an area that has many expatriates from your country. There may be many beaches with property available to buy, but only a few with large populations from your country. Just like that you have narrowed down the locations to search in, and you've done it according to your own preferences rather than the selling points of a website or forum.

You can get even more specific if you'd like. Do you want to have a view of the sea? Have a house on a golf course? Be within walking distance of the Belgian bar, the Swedish school or the British barber? All of these preferences will be on your checklist and inform the way you choose your location. (We'll get more into this in the next chapter).

The problems arise when buyers think that getting a great price is more important than the right location. Wrong, wrong, wrong.

Think about it: the wrong location will not make you happy in the long run, and if it's off the beaten track (which it well might be), you'll be stuck with it for a long time because no one else will want to buy it from you.

How much better will it be for you to spend the time to find a location you really love?

The golf resort experiment

Here's an example of a wrong location.

A luxury golf resort called Polaris World was launched with massive fanfare in 2007. Jack Nicklaus came to meet us twice to tell us how fantastic it would all be. Rumours of the Beckhams, TV celebrities and even Spanish Royalty purchasing Polaris property abounded. More incredibly, some of these stories were true. Intercontinental and a host of major European banks got involved.

Plans to build Olympic pools, four hotels, properties with helicopter landing pads, supermarkets, commercial centres, artificial football pitches, cricket pitches and eight championship golf courses were in the works.

We were getting a new airport, the biggest theme park in Europe, direct flights from the U.S. and Asia, motorways in every direction, and millions pumped into the project every day.

Then, suddenly, the investment dried up, leaving us with only a handful of buyers who wanted to live there, and nobody who wanted to invest there.

It turned out that living on the coast near to the beach was way more appealing than owning golf property. Soon Polaris World filed for bankruptcy and it was all over. (In fairness to the company Polaris did try to work their way out of the situation and now is back up and running again).

The bust could have been the end of the story. Today however golf property is making a comeback not because it's trendy, but because it's cheap. Prices have dropped 60% on golf resorts across Spain, attracting people who love golf and don't need a view of the sea. Maybe Polaris World could have avoided the bust entirely had its developers been more location-conscious in the first place.

Today these 65m2, two bedroom new apartments are perfect for our golfer clients and investors – Northern European buyers in particular. Those guys love golf, don't necessarily need to see the sea and love a bargain.

My point being – everyone's perfect location is different in Spain. Do your checklist and it will very quickly become evident where you should buy.

While you're considering locations, here are some areas to avoid:

- Places where your mobile phone does not work

- Places where there is no internet

- High crime areas

- In or near outdoor markets (imagine parking!)

- Beside the airport, or even on the flight path (yes, it's nice to be able to walk to your flight but it makes sleeping difficult. Ditto with fire and police stations).

- Beside the motorway – chances are sleep will also be difficult

- Beside the 24 hour foam party night club – again, forget sleep

- Places with crumbling infrastructure. You want the roads and bridges you drive on to be safe and in good condition, right?

You can add all of these location requirements to your checklist. In the next chapter, we'll talk more about this checklist—how to make it, why to make it, and how to make sure you stick to it.

Chapter review:

- The perfect area for one client may be the wrong area for you.

- Polaris World and other similar developments were *almost* perfect.

Chapter Eight:
Make Your List, Check it Twice

In this chapter:

- You must write an " I want list". This is non negotiable.

- You have got to know exactly what you desire if you are to be in the top 20% of successful buyers.

In order to make sure you find the right property for you, you need to know exactly what you want. And to do that, you need to make the checklist we've been talking about for a couple of chapters now. The checklist is a 20% task which gives 80% results.

You will need a pen and sheet of paper, nothing more.

Yes, you need to write this list down. Here's why.

Brian Tracy in *"The Psychology of Achievement"* tells us writing things down will give you focus. When you write things down, it frees up space in your brain—a vital commodity when choosing a new home in Spain amongst all the chaos of your property search. It's easy to get caught up in unimportant stuff like the colour of the curtains while missing out on your 80% - the price, the condition, the location and the property itself.

Similarly, David Allen in his classic productivity book *Getting Things Done* says the human brain can only hold 6 thoughts at any one time. By writing things down, you think clearer and are less prone to "brain fog."

A handwritten goal is a powerful reminder of what you want. When you use the first person (for example, "I want three bedrooms") it's even more powerful. Becoming better acquainted with yourself in this process is a huge step. When you actually write down what you want, you may find out surprising things about those desires and priorities. Your brain can play tricks on you, pen and paper will not.

Writing things on your checklist allows you to track what you've already achieved. Every box you tick is a step closer to finding the property you want.

Finally, it's possible that the dream property you want does not exist. If you are crystal clear on what you want but can't find it anywhere, you may have found a need to reevaluate what you want. This may not be fun, but it will be helpful!

Here are some things to make sure you consider as you make your checklist:

The House

- What's my absolute maximum budget?

- What's my minimum budget?

- What are my stretch budget amounts between those two?

- Number of bedrooms desired

- Number of bathrooms desired

- Size of the house (small, medium, family size, large, mansion).

- Plot size (small, medium, large)

- Pool, yes/no (consider the cost, maintenance and safety considerations as well as pool fun)

- Orientation (do you want an east-facing bedroom or a south-facing house?)

- Condition of the house (does it need to be pristine or are you okay with a fixer-upper?)

- Furnished or unfurnished?

- Garden/lawn/landscaping

The Location

- Is the area safe?

- Is it close to a medical centre?

- Is it in a walking neighborhood or will you need a car?

- What important amenities are nearby (pub, shopping, barber, spa, market, etc.)?

- Is the house close to nature?

- What is parking like? Traffic? Noise?

- Do I need to be within walking distance of the sea?

- How close to the airport or train station?

- What else do I want to be close to or far away from?

- Why am I buying here? Rental or personal?

The Deal

- Have I found an established agent?

- Have I seen some testimonials from him? (Minimum three)

- Have I called one or more of the references the agent has given me?

- Do I have a plan on how to approach this sale and is the agent a part of it?

- If I see the right house, am I prepared to pay a non-refundable deposit and sign a contract on the spot, or will I need time to consider?

- Am I prepared to walk away and not buy if I don't see the right house?

- Am I expecting to fall in love with the house, or is this a business deal?

- Do I understand a third party close?

- Will I be happy to allow someone else to negotiate on my behalf, or do I want to do it myself?

- Am I getting financing and is it ready to go and pre-approved, or do I have to go looking for a mortgage after finding the house? (Not having financing in place will cost you money at negotiation stage.)

As you answer these questions, you will start to put together a list of what you absolutely want and what is ultimately less important. You may also think of things not addressed here—by all means include them! This is your checklist.

Basic list

- Price

- Number of bedrooms. 1. 2. 3. 4. 5. 6 or more

- Number of bathrooms. 1. 2. 3. 4. 5. 6 or more

Size

- Apartment

- Semi or Duplex

- Detached villa

Cross off below what's not important and circle anything that's very important to you.

Location

- Schools

- Walking distance to the sea

- Golf

- Safe area

- Established area

- Bars restaurants

- Supermarket

- Medical centre

The House

- Enclosed garden

- Lawns

- Pool

- Garage

- Condition

- Air conditioning

- Adequate furniture and appliances

- Outstanding furniture and appliances

- Wifi area

Other

1

2

3

4

5

(For example; hot tub, landscaped gardens, whatever is important to you)

The only way to 100% ensure that you buy the right property is to write a checklist and stick to it. This step in purchasing a property in Spain cannot be overlooked.

If you skip this, you statistically will not buy the right house for you. In over two thousand real estate deals, I and my team have seen close to 60% of customers buy what ultimately turned out to be the wrong property, simply because they did not bother to make a checklist and stick to it.

And don't forget the "stick to it" part! You will be influenced by a crafty salesman who tries to sell you the house with the bigger commission, by people you meet in the bar who tell you that you'd love to be where they are, even though it's not where you really want to be, or even by sudden impulses your brain gives you...

Everyone's checklist is different, but everyone's need to stick to theirs is the same.

In Summer 2014, a lovely Irish couple came to La Zenia, Spain to buy and were introduced to me by Sean, one of my salesmen. We discovered we had friends in common and they decided to work with us to find their new property.

They wanted something less than 80,000 euro within walking distance of the sea. Their 8-year-old daughter wanted a communal pool. The mother was anxious for the complex to be safe and secure for when she would come on her own. Neither of them intended to drive while they were here. They expressed an interest in being close to the supermarkets, bars, restaurants etc.

We had just listed a south-facing two-bedroom apartment, overlooking the communal pool, right in the heart of La Zenia, a full 10,000 below their upper purchasing limit.

They viewed it and loved it.

Sean naturally advised them to go have a coffee and a think before they put pen to paper. Strangely they called him back and said they would delay the purchase until the next morning. Apparently, as well as meeting with us, they also had arranged to meet a guy who "did a bit of selling on the side" and was introduced to them by an acquaintance back home.

This agent showed them a three-bedroom house on a golf course. Now, from chatting with this couple I knew neither of them played golf. The house was also half an hour's drive to the sea – basically in the middle of nowhere. But the price had just been reduced by 20,000 that day to only 95,000 euro.

The clients called us next day to say the deal was off on the La Zenia apartment; they were buying this house instead.

We could not believe it, so I called them back and asked them to reconsider for their own sake. It was all the same to me. I almost never call back a client when they have made their mind up and immediately I regretted it.

They told me that their decision was made; they had often talked about taking up golf, the agent was not charging them a commission, the furniture was fantastic, with the new motorway they could drive to the beach in 25 minutes, they could borrow the extra money from the credit union and the price was down to 95,000 euro.

What could I do? I wished them well and we probably will never hear from them again.

Now, what happened here? I don't know the whole story, but it sounded to me like these clients ran afoul of an illegal agent, or at least a salesman who did a great job of selling them a house that didn't match with the preferences they told Sean and me about. More importantly, as far as I could tell they did not have a written checklist that they were committed to sticking to (they certainly never showed me one), and as a result they bought a house that was very different than the desired property they described to me.

Was that house the wrong house for them? I have no idea. For all I know they could have really fallen in love with it, and been willing to give up the beach access, community pool, and non-driving neighborhood for it. But my guess is that their lack of a checklist is what made them look at such a different house to begin with. If they'd had a written checklist and stuck to it, they'd have seen right off how strong a match for them the La Zenia apartment was, and never looked at a house so different from it.

Your checklist can take any form. You can use the questions here to inspire you or make one up for yourself. But make sure you make one and stick to it! Without one, you run an immense risk of buying the wrong house. With one, you will likely find the perfect property before you view three houses.

Chapter review:

- Feeling listless? Then write a list. Its the first key to success.

- The format of your list is unimportant, just write down what you want and what you don't.

- If you have no list, no written guidelines, you are at the mercy of any smooth talking salesman.

Chapter Nine:
Where Does it all go Wrong for Buyers in Spain?

In this chapter:

- There are three people who can mess this up. Who are they?

- Who are the bad agents to deal with?

- What's the downside to a bad agent. (One of the 80%, as opposed to the 20% of good ones).

Before we can explain how you can improve your chances you must know how 80% of the mistakes are made.

There are only three parties who can mess this process up:

- The agent

- The buyer (that's you!)

- The seller

We're going to talk about each of these in the next three chapters.

First - The Agent

People sometimes ask me: "do I actually need an agent?" My reply is always the same: "do you cut your own hair?"

Agents are here to make the real estate transaction simple and painless. Why would you _not_ want to use one if you find one you can trust? The only reasons are lack of understanding of what the agent does or feeling you know more than the agent does, which we'll talk about in the next chapter.

So, first things first, when buying property in a foreign country, GET AN AGENT. Later we will explain how to get this agent on your side of the deal, but we need to find them first. Ask yourself: is this the kind of person I'd want to **sell** my house? If so, that means they probably have the listings you need. If not, probably they are not the agent you are looking for.

If you are dealing with a bank in Spain or anywhere, make sure you do it through a buffer who knows what they are doing and do not assume that the bank knows anything or cares less about you.

Today in Spain you can buy from a number of different kinds of agents:

- A registered agent or agency

- Privately from a builder or developer

- Privately from an individual seller

- A "street agent," who has no office or company

- A part time agent who has another job or business (often owns a shop or bar) but sells houses on the side

- The bank

20% work for 80% return is to find an agent who is dealing directly with the owner/builder/bank/developer and trust them to do their job. But since this chapter is about how some agents can mess up your house buying process, here are a few agents to avoid at all costs:

- **The agent who does not listen.** You tell your guy you are interested in a two-bed walking distance to the sea. He starts by showing you a three-bed well outside your budget ten miles from the beach. This is not the salesperson for you.

- **The agent who is passing through.** Typically this agent will drive a foreign car, does not have family in the country and rents rather than owns their home in Spain. Watch this guy, he is likely to take your deposit, stick it in his glove compartment and disappear overnight.

- **The poser.** This agent is more interested in their image as a real estate agent than actually getting you the deal you deserve. They want you to know how wonderful they are. They will tell you stories of their (useless) degrees, heaps of experience, knowledge of the laws of the land, their popularity and hundreds of Facebook fans. Their only concern is themselves and how they look to their new friends and people from their hometown who follow them on Facebook. None of this helps you.

- **The abusive agent.** If your agent starts telling you that they are used to dealing with clients who have a higher budget that you or that the last client they had made his mind up in two hours, or any more passive-aggressive behavior, it's time to break up. They will often appear distant when you ask them a real question, as they know the real answer is not what you want to hear.

- **The unethical agent.** As we tell our clients all the time, you don't have to love us, or even like us, but you will get the best deal from us. If your agent is spending too much time befriending you, buying you beers, being overly generous, they may be trying to hide something - like their inability to do the job.

- **The betrayer.** Judas will tell the owner that you *really* like that house or maybe that you can stretch your budget a further 10% - without consulting you first. This makes them popular with the seller but costs you money. Another part of this is full disclosure. If the owner is a family friend for example you need to know that. The agent should only get one chance to come clean up front. If you find out they've been dishonest or only partially truthful, drop them immediately.

- **The inexperienced agent.** If you are buying through a mid-size agency you can get away with this as an inexperienced agent has a good support structure. But if the agent is working solo and you're his very first client? Do you think they will know the region, understand that new tax law, have the correct contacts, understand the market trends? Probably not. Be careful.

- **Pushy or non-pushy.** Clients hate pushy sales people, yet people buy from pushy sales people all the time. *"There is another buyer about to pay the deposit, if you want it you'd better sign the contract now… it's the last house for sale in Spain"*. This sales pitch works, but only in favor of the agent. Bad news for buyers. Avoid this guy. Almost as bad is the non-pushy sales agent. This agent takes his time doing his job and often needs you to remind him to work on your behalf. If you make an offer on a property, the agent must call the seller that second. If you need to chase him down to find out what he's doing, and when you do that you find out he still has not got around to making the offer and he does not want to disturb the owner, it's time to find a more pushy agent. There's a middle ground between these two agents. Find it.

- **The agent who has no time.** You are calling and calling your agent but there's no reply. Right, it's time to look elsewhere. Either they spend too much time napping or have too many clients – either way, it's bad news for you.

- **The broke estate agent.** You may be tempted to feel sorry for your broke estate agent. After all, its not her fault; her lawyer screwed her, her ex husband got everything, her last boss was an ass, the economy, the long evenings, the dog is having puppies, cute lovely puppies, and now you were wondering could you trust her. A broke salesperson is a dangerous thing-desperation drives people to focus on their commission and not your needs. Dangerous. And finally…

- *The "I'm not really committed to this business, but I like the commissions" agent. These can include:*

  - The local newspaper

  - The bank manager

  - The guy working in the charity shop up the road

  - The guy from the Argentinian restaurant

  - The presidents of most of the communities around here

  - The golf pro at the local course

  - The bar man in the Spanish cafe.

These are the "street agents" and part time agents we talked about above. These guys are not in the real estate business officially but they are tempted to get involved by the C word - **commissions.**

Up to 20% of sales in Spain (there are no official figures) are orchestrated by unofficial estate agents.

What will they do to help you if something goes wrong with the sale? What do they know about it?

Again there are no official figures as to how many of the sales that go wrong are the fault of non-estate agents getting involved, but going on my 80/20 rule, I'm guessing 80% of mistakes are made by these people.

In Spain in 2014 there is something in the region of **30,000 estate agents** working in the industry. That is a lot of estate agents. And many of these are the uncommitted, unlicensed, unregistered, unsupported salespeople described in this item. They aren't bad people. But they don't have the knowledge base or the expertise or the motivation to get you the best deal on the right property.

Think about it. The bar man may be genuinely trying to help you. Perhaps he is trying to help his cousin out who can't sell his apartment. Do either of them have the necessary expertise to get the deal closed? Can we trust them with a deposit? Generally not – usually these are the deals least likely to ever complete.

The guy who owns the shop around the corner, or the local newspaper/barber shop is another terrible place to start your search for a property. What can these guys add to the sector? Generally just confusion, doubt and a bad deal.

They have no houses listed on their books. Often they just introduce buyers to a proper agent in exchange for a commission without the buyer actually knowing what just happened. That extra fee gets tacked onto the price that you, the buyer, end up paying. That's right, going through one of these non-agent agents will cost you *more* money, not less.

On top of that, solo agents can't have the same level of knowledge as a large company. How can one person know as much as all of them? They can't.

Some buyers will buy directly from the developer or builder in order to save commission. Problem is, if they went to an agent they would pay the same price and get loads of extras (we throw in white kitchen goods, maybe free legal fees, perhaps a year's free property management and generally a refund on the commission we receive). Also, if you buy through a respected agent you have some serious clout. If there is a problem your agent will be able to help the builder fix it for you. All of this and it costs you absolutely nothing extra.

A note on "For sale by owner" deals: as a rule of thumb worldwide, just 10% of deals which are done privately or "FSBO" actually complete. Just 10% and still we see sellers in Spain advertising their house for sale "with no commission". This is not a good way to sell your house, as the odds of success are against you. It doesn't work.

Finally, some buyers go directly to the bank and believe that they will save the commission that way. This also is counterproductive. Agents sell the same properties as the bank for the exact same price. You might think that the price of a bad debt or repossession is the final, firm price. Absolutely not.

Good agents can negotiate price reductions on repossessions of 10, 20 or maybe 30%. Yet buyers sometimes feel that if they deal face to face with bank clerk they will get the best price. These buyers cost themselves thousands every day and will never know they have done it.

Just a few facts on the banks, now the largest property owners in Spain, to make you think before you buy directly from them.

Since the financial crisis hit Spain, in 2008 the Spanish banks have accepted rescue loans in the region of 100,000 million euro.

Originally they refused loans from the ECB stating that they could work their way out of the crisis themselves, in conjunction with regional governments. It later emerged that they were totally insolvent, top heavy with management, partaking in risky real estate loans and funding "vanity projects" for the local governments.

They did not want anyone looking at their books and that was the reason for their reluctance to take the bailout.

Look at Corvera Airport or any one of the 30 airports in Spain which have been completed and have yet to have a commercial plane touch down on tarmac there.

Most of these will never open. They were vanity projects dreamed up by mayors and councillors in small country regions where there is no need for an airport. This was done in conjunction with the very people clients are trusting to sell them property, The Spanish banks!

Finally in order to save the banking system, (Spain is one of the biggest economies in Europe with German, British and even Irish banks having billions of euro tied up in them) 60% of the smaller banks were disbanded and 40,000 employees lost their jobs in the sector.

This is interesting... The number of managers and middle managers who lost their jobs due to restructure or mismanagement = Zero.

It has been said, (not by me as clarified by my lawyer when he read this paragraph) that there was a fear that senior bank officials who were laid off or charged with fraud would talk of the malpractice within the Spanish banking industry and its close relationship to Spanish Government. They were paid off in exchange for their silence regarding banking fraud, it has been claimed.

Banks appear to be on the road to recovery yet the system still lacks transparency.

Despite all the damning evidence clients every day walk into their local branch and buy a "repossession" believing that the bank knows what it is doing and they have the best interests of the client at heart.

Bottom line, you should never buy a repossession house from the bank without the assistance of a property professional.

For the buyer who picks any type of bad agent the result will be the same:

- You will pay too much for the house.

- You will likely buy the wrong house.

- Resale will be tough and expensive.

- The whole buying experience will be long, costly, stressful and ultimately it will be a negative time for you and your family.

A word of warning: You need to be aware of incentive caused bias. i.e. An agent pushing you in the direction of a deal you don't like because it suits them to do so.

Chapter review:

- Who are the three parties in this deal who can mess it up for the buyer?

- What does a bad estate agent look like?

- If your agent is not in the top 20% of estate agents in Spain, whats the loss to you?

- The banks: The largest owner of property in Spain. Do they know what they are doing?

Chapter Ten:
Your Own Worst Enemy.

In this chapter:

- How do we as investors mess things up?

- Risk aversion

- "Its written in the stars"

- Human brain traps.

- Anchoring

- Sunk costs

- Confirmation trap

- Situation blindness

- Relativity trap

- Superiority trap

That's right. This chapter is all about you, the buyer. Since you're reading this book, you're probably pretty smart. But even the smartest people can mess up.

This chapter is meant to forewarn you of many of the ways that can happen, so you can avoid and prevent them when you go to buy your house. Even if you think this chapter might not apply to you, read it anyway. At the very least you'll learn some important things about your worst enemy: your brain.

"The buyer's worst enemy is often the buyer" Ian Comaskey

Your brain reacts to many things when signing the real estate deal. The colour of the walls, the Aloe Vera tree in the driveway, how much you like the estate agent, even how attractive the agent is.

Think you're not swayed by an attractive agent? Think again.

Michael Seiler, University of Norfolk. Va. has found that buyers are more susceptible to the attractiveness of the estate agent. The more attractive the agent the more the buyer is likely to pay.

It makes great TV to see the elderly English couple telling the reporter through teary eyes that they have lost everything because of an unscrupulous builder in Spain, an agent who didn't do her job or a shady bank/town-hall/mortgage broker. But what a TV presenter must want to do is to grab them by the shoulders and shake them repeating *"what were you thinking, what were you thinking!"*

We don't like to say it, but these mini disasters are the fault of the *client*, not the con man who stole their money. The con artist is simply doing his job. The buyers did not, however, do theirs.

It's the same on a smaller scale when buyers pay too much or just buy the wrong house. It's no good saying that they were pressured into making a hasty decision by the sales guy. It's useless to claim that the builder promised that he would finish the communal pool or the bank promised them a good deal on their mortgage.

Claiming it's not like this at home in Belgium or Finland is equally fruitless. The system here is the way it is. Sales people here are the way they are. It's up to *you* to protect your investment. Nobody cares about your purchase in Spain as much as you do. The fame you'll get on TV is not worth the stress of losing your cash and your time.

So if all these disastrous sales situations are our own faults, why do we keep ending up in them?

It all comes back to the brain. Remember, your brain is your worst enemy! Specifically, there are several habits of thought that are so ingrained they are almost unconscious, and five psychological traps that your brain is hardwired to fall into. These brain issues are at the root of at least 80% of the mistakes that lead to the kinds of situations we just talked about.

So let's talk about these traps, so you don't have to fall victim to them when you come to buy your house.

Risk Aversion

Most people are risk averse. Risk aversion means wanting to be safe and avoid risk at all costs. In this context, it shows up as preferring to avoid a loss than to acquire a gain, making a safe choice over a risky one.

The great majority of Europeans and therefore the great majority of Spanish property buyers strongly prefer avoiding losses to acquiring gains. Some experts tell us that risk aversion is so strong that we get double the pain when we lose money as opposed to the pleasure of gaining the exact same amount. None of us want to lose money, even when faced with the possibility of making even more if we take a risk.

Any agent may tell you that they can save you 10,000 euro. The fear of losing a 3,000 euro deposit can be too great however even for what appears to be a no lose situation. One of the reasons for this fear is the amount of negativity that the media vomits regularly about real estate professionals in Spain. It's bad enough that the press writes about this but British TV loves the sad story of the unfortunate couple that lost their life savings while buying in Spain.

The fact they bought from a dodgy-looking Colombian who met them in an industrial unit and who insisted on taking cash only is not that big of a part of the story apparently!

On top of that there are a thousand ex-pat forums where disgruntled clients can rant anonymously about their agent, lawyer or sales professional. These forums are just septic tanks for complainers to do their job of complaining but can often frighten buyers into making the wrong decision.

Is it any wonder clients are nervous when parting with their cash?

Risk aversion is strong. We should be aware of it's existence yet not feed it unnecessarily. Do your research on your agent, fill in your checklist and you have little to fear.

If it is to be, it is up to me.

"If it's for you, it won't pass you by" goes the old saying.

Unfortunately when it comes to buying property in Spain that is rubbish!

I've heard this sort of thing more than you can imagine.

A client tells me, "Well if the seller will not drop his price to 100,000 euro, then it's just not meant to be." What? Seriously?

Okay, sometimes things go wrong in life and in buying a house. Sometimes the owner changes the goalposts, or changes the price before he signs the house over to you. This happens to every one of us. We just start all over again. But to say that you are not buying because it's not meant to be, or the tea-leaves told you not to is hocus-pocus.

It's also the complete opposite to what the great Brian Tracy, businessman and author says in the classic, "*The Psychology of Achievement.*"

"If it's to be, it's up to me".

It's not up to anyone else to get the deal done; it's up to me. That is, YOU.

A buyer this time last year, came to Spain and came specifically to our firm. He had just received 100,000 in a retirement deal from the Irish Government agency that he recently took retirement from.

He had a very decent pension for the rest of his life from the Irish state – he was in good financial shape. Like so many of our buyers, Pat had paid his dues and wanted a little place in the sun where he, his family and especially his grandkids could come and have summer vacation time.

He came to talk to us.

We found the right house, I mean perfect: Three bedroom overlooking the pool, walking distance to the beach, enclosed community so that the kids would always be safe. Because it's in La Zenia our sales team told him that he could never lose money at this price. His wife loved it. It gets better: the owners wanted a quick sale and would move out in time for Pat to get the summer holidays with his family – his first summer as a retiree.

Problem was, a friend of his who read an article online told Pat never to offer the asking price when negotiating in Spain. So Pat made an offer well below the price. The owners didn't like the offer and refused. Pat said he'd meet them halfway, still miles below asking price. We assured him that the offer would not work and it didn't.

There were plenty of viewings, the owners knew they would sell, but now Pat was saying "Well, if it's not meant to be…" We assured him and so did his wife that it was meant to be – just pay the asking price, still saving money and get the house he wanted. He had 24 hours to think about it but stuck to his guns – Fate was telling him they would drop the price eventually.

He refused to budge, the owners got a better offer from another agent within days. Pat missed out on the house he should have bought.

So, you waited a day too long and someone else bought the house before you got to pay your deposit.

That's your fault, not the fault of the stars. You were too slow. That's okay though! Now get back up and buy your number two choice.

Don't make the mistake Pat made. There are many reasons to not buy a property in Spain, but fate need not be one. If it's to be, it's up to YOU!

<u>The Traps</u>

The human brain is a funny thing. It's amazing how it can fool us in all walks of life.

Many of us play golf. We line up the putt to drop right into the hole 6 feet away. We take a practice putt. We "see" it falling into the cup, we steady ourselves for the putt, draw back the putter and just as the club face is about to strike the ball, our brain tells our hand, "that's not the line."

What happens then? Your hand twists uncontrollably and you miss the 6 footer. Not a word of apology from the brain, but you rush out next day to buy a new driver to compensate.

Think about that. Because of this brain issue Ping and Nike have made billions selling drivers and irons to people who missed a 6 foot putt.

And so it is when it comes to making a large purchase. We must be aware of the story our brain is telling us and how it differs from the reality of the situation.

There are 6 main traps the brain will fall into just like it does with the missed tap-in.

1. Anchoring

We humans get fixed ideas in our heads. We become anchored to these ideas that we have and believe them despite evidence to the contrary. You see this a lot in politics: members of one party tend anchor to the idea that their party is right and good and the other party is wrong and evil, end of discussion. And they hold to that belief even when the other party does something clearly good or right.

In the Spanish real estate context, we see dramatic stories in the tabloids telling us how dangerous it is to buy property in Spain. "Spain to introduce new tax on Irish people"; "Economy in Spain in Free fall"; "Houses for free in Spain". None of these headlines are helpful and in fact they are very negative for potential buyers; often costing them the chance to buy the property they wanted.

What that does for buyers very often is anchor the belief that there is a good chance that if they go to buy a property in Spain, everyone there will be out to get them.

Some clients will "protect themselves" in their heads, by only buying from native Spanish agents while in reality the Irish, English, Scandinavian and sometimes Russian agents are the ones who are most trusted in the area. They are the ones who came to the market originally with "new eyes" and therefore they are the ones with the knowledge and skills that buyers need. But buyers anchored to the idea of buying from Spanish agents will hurt themselves because of it.

Remember how sometimes buyers buy direct from banks? Why? Well, they know they can trust the banks more than they can trust real estate agents. This is an anchoring trap that we all somehow still believe.

Bank officials are good people as a general rule. The problem is not the individuals themselves. Bank staff should not be trying to sell property no more than I should be selling credit cards. It's not their job and its unfair to ask them to do so. Worse still for the relatively small number of bank staff, who actually know how to sell things, the system the banks insist on using means the deck is firmly stacked against them. For years now I have said to the banks that if they got out of our way we could sell all of their stock of property. There are other clear reasons why this will never happen and the Spanish tax payer as well as the property buyer are footing the bill.

Do all banks engage in various kind of fraud? Are all agents as honest as we are? No and no. But many buyers are anchored to the belief that you can and should automatically trust the banks, not trust your estate agent and it's just not true.

To avoid anchoring (in life), you must be open to new sources of information. A financial tsunami may be just over the horizon and in order to be ready, be flexible in your thinking.

Stick to the best sources of real information – information relevant to you and your situation. Ask questions and allow time to digest the answers. Consider that you might be wrong; that the way you've always thought about or done something might be better another way.

2. Sunk Costs

Psychologists tell us the reason we stay in bad relationships way beyond the sell by date is due to "sunk costs." We've invested this much time, we are not jumping ship now. Buyers are often the same with estate agents.

Believe me, many people should have walked away from their agent long before now but, well, "We've invested this much time with her, our kids are the same age, my cousins bought through her…"

There are 50 ways to leave your lover and just as many ways to leave your agent. If you need to do it, do it.

Similarly, I know people who have invested so much time and love into their dream home that they just can't walk away from it even when it's become a disaster.

They have told their friends how great it is. They talk about it on Facebook. They have new friends who also bought there. They love it, although they know it's costing them a fortune and they probably should never have bought it in the first place. They know they should give up, but they've put so much in that they won't listen to reason.

For buyers, you must know when its time to walk away. I've seen clients pay a deposit for a property and then realize it was not the one for them. Knowing that they'd lose their 3,000 euro deposit, they stayed involved in the deal and ended up settling for a property they did not want.

The most dangerous time for buyers who are on inspection trips is the last few hours. They start to think, especially if the salesman is any good, that they have invested four days of their lives looking at houses and not found the right one. It's so easy to make a bad decision rather than just "waste" the four days we've already invested.

We had a client towards the end of 2012, a teacher from England, who got into a situation that illustrates the sunk cost fallacy perfectly.

We found her the right house but so did another agent. The owner understandably thought he had two buyers, as both agents approached him to get his best price.

The other agents came back to her first, maybe in good faith, and said, more or less "you have to buy it at the asking price, there is another buyer ready to buy it today". Not realizing that she herself was the other buyer, she panicked and paid a 3,000 deposit.

Meanwhile our agent had negotiated the owner down by 10,000 euro, he needed a quick sale and if the "other buyer" didn't buy it, he'd take our lady's offer.

Get it? One buyer, two different prices negotiated by two different agents on the same property. What a mess!

We met with the lady and told her the story. You'd imagine she would be delighted, but no. She said that she had already paid a deposit and was not prepared to lose it. We explained that she would save 10,000 anyway and come out 7,000 euro ahead.

She refused and bought at the higher price as she did not want to lose the money she had already paid. For the sake of saving her sunk costs 3,000 euro, she threw away more than twice as much.

3. Confirmation Trap

Having already married ourselves to our sunk costs, we as buyers and investors look for peers who are going to tell us we have made the right decision. We hang around on forums and talk to people who will agree with us, not question us.

I've had this conversation more times than I can remember.

We love to follow the crowd, even us solo entrepreneurs and investors. At some stage in the process we must face the same way as the crowd or we can't hope to make a profit from the deal. We convince ourselves it's less of a gamble and at worst speculating, the more people we see do it. This is how the stock market works, everyone is buying a certain stock so it must make sense?

Everyone is buying in Turkey so that must be the place to buy, right? Sometimes this can be the right thing to do but as in the Dutch Tulip bubble of 1637 or any of the various stock crashes since 1987, following the herd can get you in a lot of trouble.

I have an uncle who loves his confirmations.

When changing his car a few years back he wanted a BMW but was struggling to justify the price tag. What he did was ask everyone he knew the same question. "If you were changing your car tomorrow, what would you buy?"

The Toyota, Smart car and Mazda answers were quickly forgotten every time someone would suggest a BMW. When someone did not suggest his favourite German motor he would prompt them with "Well, Pat said I should go for a BMW". Guess what, the answer he received would change.

If you ask the question often enough, you'll get the answer you are looking for!

He bought a BMW.

When making a big decision like buying a property, take the time to explore and consider opinions, especially expert opinions that are different than yours. Even if you end up making the same decision, you'll have considered it more carefully and know you're making it for the right reasons.

4. Situational Blindness

This is when we subconsciously use our brains to hide some information from ourselves. Why? Because it's easier to ignore information we don't like than to face it.

We know that the car salesman is telling us a few little white lies. The SUV is probably harder on diesel than what he is saying.

We are pretty sure the costs of running the pool are more than the agent has told us.

We know we are not getting a great deal. "It's an okay deal and what's an extra 5,000 euro over 10 years anyway."

We know that buying next to a construction site isn't a good idea. *"They will probably finish that golf course eventually."*

We shut out what we know deep down to be true. It is much easier in the short term and we can postpone the evil day when we must financially face facts that.

We should not have bought that house.

(BTW – they won't finish the golf course, the builder is bankrupt.)

5. Relativity trap

We saw this every day during the crazy years of Spanish real estate in 2004-2008. Clients forgot that they were investing for themselves, and their specific situation, nobody else. People watched what other people were buying and forgot what they were there to do.

They overspent because some relation or co-worker of theirs was buying a bigger place than what they had picked out. They bought in the wrong area and for the wrong reason.

A buyer named Mary came to us to purchase a small apartment in 2006, prices were rising and she didn't want to miss the property boat. She had 90,000 euro in cash and that just about got her the property she wanted for her and the family.

Unfortunately, somewhere in the process she met an agent who turned her into a gambler while telling her she was an investor. I'm skipping a few steps but Mary finally bought from us, mortgaged half the property and bought from the other guy as well.

Her fear of missing out on the appreciation on two houses was greater than the common sense of buying one. She wasn't alone, far from it and needless to say, her 2nd purchase proved to be a mistake.

6. Superiority Trap

The most cunning trap our brain has set for us is the idea that we know everything. We know more than the politicians, weathermen and even soccer pundits on Sky Sports. (Actually we probably do know more than the soccer pundits).

In other words, we feel that we know more than the experts. You were pretty smart at school, right? You've got common sense? Then you should know how to buy property for yourself? Worse still, the more PHD's and MBA's we have beside our name, the more likely we are to get basic investing wrong.

We are overconfident and that leads to mistakes, big ones. The minute details of the purchase are genuinely boring, and that leads to disaster.

Did you know that dentists have the least amount of assets on retirement relative to what they have earned over their lifetime? That means they lose more money than any other profession. Second place are doctors, a very close second.

There are several reasons for this:

- Due to the very nature of their job, they can't really talk to their clients so they end up making a lot of decisions on their own. It's hard to get advice from the agent you have in the chair as you stick needles into his gums.

- They were in many cases the smartest kid in the class so their friends asked them stuff, not the other way around – they didn't copy their friend's homework like I did.

- It's a lot easier to buy a property in Spain than perform a root canal extraction.

- When they come to Spain or wherever they intend to purchase their second home, they go it alone. They have not developed the instinct to find a great estate agent and trust him.

- They do not take the time to write a checklist but due to their intelligence they will try to hold the information in their heads.

- If we think we are more informed than we really are then we take shortcuts and get caught up in the stuff that does not matter, missing out on the stuff that does. Every single one of us is guilty of this.

It is the central property of suckers that they will never know they were suckers.

Conclusion

These psychological traps will catch buyers of products and services in every single country in the world every single day, sometimes with disastrous consequences.

Con men thrive on the flaws our brains have installed on our hard drives. Even with the best intentions, we want the deal to be exactly what we want it to be. Well, it's not. We shut out reality, fail to concentrate on what we are good at and we seek the comfort of finding other victims while failing to be honest with ourselves.

To avoid these traps you or rather we, must be aware of their existence. We have to know that we are not immune to their influence. We have to seek professional advice, tell ourselves that cutting our own hair makes no sense, be realistic, and write it down.

Write everything down.

That's your 80/20 right there.

Chapter review:

- You are the biggest danger to getting this process right and it's not your fault- It's your brain that's to blame.

- Psychological traps exist whether we believe them or not.

- Just like gravity, they influence us without us ever knowing.

- The smarter you are, the bigger influence human brain traps have on you.

Chapter Eleven:
Sellers and Selling

In this chapter:

- Sellers are not necessarily business people. Don't treat them like a client.

- Many sellers have lost a lot of money over the last few years- maybe they are sore about that.

- You have got to respect the seller in order to get the deal you want.

- What is a buffer and could I need one?

Finally, we have the seller.

I'd love to say that sellers are easy; they list a property for a fair price, listen to offers, accept the offer they like, take the property off the market and do everything they can to make the move as seamless as possible for the new owner of the property.

The day before the completion they are frantically cleaning the house so it will be pristine for the new owners. They fill the fridge, buy an expensive bottle of bubbly and create a fantastic feeling for both them and the new buyer

Well, that does happen sometimes, once or twice maybe in the couple of thousand deals I've done. But sellers can cause as many problems as bad agents or your own brain's traps.

The way to ensure that the deal gets done without any issues from the seller is to become a salesperson, even if only for the duration of this process.

Truth is we are all salespeople. Do you think if you are trying to get finance for a home purchase from the local bank you are not selling yourself to the bank manager? You are! What about meeting a new love interest in one of those trendy online dating sites? *(Do you imagine some of these "recent photos" might have been run though* Photoshop *a couple of times?)* We all sell when we need to.

Real estate is no different than life. Yes, we encourage our sellers to cut the grass, wash the windows or deep clean the kitchen before a viewing. We do stop just short of asking our client to put bread into the oven or have the smell of coffee wafting through the house. What's wrong with showing a potential buyer the best side of the house? Well, nothing.

It works the same way with you as the buyer. Sell yourself to the agent, and sell yourself to the owner of the property.

Let the agent know you are not kicking tyres or banging walls – if he shows you the right house you will buy it. Tell him that.

Be willing to view only at times that suit the seller. When the deal is struck, have the deposit there and then. Don't quibble over the broken garden furniture or the microwave. If they want to take it allow them.

Remember that money is not the only thing that gets a deal across the line.

I had a buyer once pay a home owner two months overdue mortgage payments at a cost of 1,000 euro, in order to get a 5,000 reduction in the price. It suited the seller because the buyer sold the idea to him.

Be flexible, be nice; sell yourself.

George Clooney is one of the best examples of this practice I know.

Today he is one of the most famous actors in the world, but it was not always like that for him.

Truth was, George could not get a job until he became a salesman. His good looks and charm got him auditions – tons of them – but still for years he could not land a decent part until he realized he was doing it all wrong.

One day he thought, "I have to stop going to auditions hoping they like me. I have to start thinking I am the answer to their problems".

He became a salesman and sold his benefits to TV series and movie producers like few before him. Before every audition he thought to himself, "What do they want from me? How will I provide it?"

Imagine the difference it would make to the process of buying the right home in Spain if instead of trying to beat the seller in negotiation or pull a fast one on your agent, you thought, "What does this person need? Can I be the answer to her problems?"

You are a buyer, with money. They are a house seller, with a problem. She is an estate agent looking to close a deal, that's her job. It's a match made in heaven.

Become the answer to people's problems - not just another one of them.

<u>What is a Buffer?</u>

The first thing an estate agent does is act as a buffer for you, the property buyer. An estate agent's aim is to reach agreement between a buyer and a seller.

Without common ground no sale takes place, no commission is earned and no house is sold. The chances are your seller is not a sophisticated business person. Odds are you are dealing with an older couple who have only bought or sold one property in their lives, certainly only one property in Spain, this one.

It's their pride and joy, they have bought the curtains in the UK and shipped them over especially for this house. They tell us the conservatory is the best on the whole estate. Everyone in the community says that they have the very best location there. They love the house. Really they don't want to sell but circumstances dictate that they are moving home.

Think about it: already we are dealing with someone who resents you.

Worse news is that the price of the house has dropped 150,000 euro over the past four years. This does not make closing the deal any easier.

Do you think that there is a bit of work to do on these people rather than just hitting them with a silly offer? You are dead right there is.

Firstly you have to get them to want to deal – that in itself is a challenge and one your buffer is up for.

Agents add space and time to every deal and to both buyer and   seller.
Nobody likes a gun to their head and the ability to say, "Well I need to talk to the agent", rather than rushing either side is so important. Buffers increase the chance of a deal being reached where both parties feel they got what they wanted.

How many times do you see successful sports teams lose a star player because his nose is out of joint since the arrival of the new superstar. The team and the player don't talk - so in the absence of a buffer, communication breaks down.

The right buffer will help you reach agreement with the seller.

You either directly or indirectly will gain more by selling yourself to the home owner you are trying to deal with.

You must see things from the seller's point of view, help solve their problem while being crystal clear in what you want.

A delicate balancing act, but very worthwhile for all parties concerned.

Picking your buffer is very much part of the 20% that gives you 80% results. Get it right.

Chapter review:

- There is no advantage in upsetting the seller, none.

- There are more ways to get a deal than just money.

- George Clooney became a salesman and sold himself. Maybe we should become the solution to someone else's problem.

- A buffer may be exactly what you need to reach agreement between you and the sellers.

Chapter Twelve:
Get Yourself a Buying Assistant

In this chapter:

- What is a buying assistant?

- Can this work for me?

- How do they get paid?

What if there was a way rather than having an estate agent trying to sell you something, you found yourself a "buying assistant," who had no vested interest in what you bought, they just wanted you to get the best deal? What if they put in writing that they would refund the commission in total to you on the deal? Do you think that would make buying any more fun?

Let me explain. Say, you find the company you think you'll work with. They have bags of experience, a good reputation, testimonials, agents who live in Spain and you feel you can trust them. Why not approach the agent and ask them will they work for zero commission and a flat fee instead?

Now, why would they do that?

Agents get paid anything from 3% to 7% of the sales price as a rule of thumb. In some cases more, in some cases less. .

Let's say that the total commission paid to an agent on a 500,000 deal is 25,000 euro. If you can find an agent who will operate on a 5,000 euro flat fee in advance she will refund the total commission to you, in this example saving you 20,000 euro. This practice is common in other countries like the U.S., but largely unheard of in Spain.

So, if you are looking for an assistant to hold your hand for a week, you need to pay them well. Half now, half after they find you the house.

If the agent is good at their job, not only will they save you the full commission, they should get a reduction on the price from the seller, plus save you money on legal fees, currency trade, etc. They will give you a clear breakdown of exactly how many thousands they have saved you on commissions, (currency, legal, real estate etc.) and in return all they then need is a testimonial and a promise you'll tell your friends!

This assistant is yours for the week to show you the areas, tell you exactly what you need to know about schools, hospitals and facilities. They will deal with agents and owners on your behalf. They will organise engineers' reports, builders, WIFI connection. Basically everything you need can be taken care of.

If you do buy, you pay no commission, you save thousands and everyone has had a much more positive experience. Sales lines, commissions, hard sell etc., are all off the table, it's just you working with your buying assistant.

Generally 3,000 euro per week is the absolute minimum figure you should pay. If an agent will work for less than that, I personally would not work with them. This is harsh on the poor agents just trying to get established but you are not here to make friends.

This is how we buy our personal cars here in Spain, by the way. We have an agent called Sorjen who sources suitable cars, based on our price and preference. He finds the car for us, checks the paperwork, service history and price. When he has found us the right vehicle he sends us details.

We trust him enough to not have to do any research whatsoever on the vehicle and we send him the money. Two days later our new car arrives to our house. Please email me if you want to receive contact details of our vehicle buying assistant.

Perhaps your assistant talks you *out* of buying. That too can be the best advice you can get – they are on your side. They are not working for commission so if they have a nagging feeling that something is not right, they will tell you. That's what you pay them for.

Will most buyers work with a buying assistant? Absolutely not! 3,000 euro per week is a lot of money. Not every buyer will be able to do this, and many will not want to. But if you can invest this money in a buying assistant, that assistant will save you a lot more.

An experienced buying assistant knows how to save you cash at every stage and I have often proven to buyers that doing this they will save tens of thousands.

In 2006 my uncle Fehin had a client in Spain on a viewing trip. She was a young woman who had recently been widowed. She had a lump sum to invest and did not want to miss the crest of the property wave.

The more he talked to her, the more Fehin realized that this was not the investment for her. She would have to borrow

50% of the money. Her eldest was starting in college in two years. She already had a hefty mortgage in Ireland.

Fehin, the buying assistant, advised her not to buy in Spain but to pay down her Irish mortgage. I couldn't believe he actually did this. She wanted to buy and now no sale meant no commission but of course he was right.

Unfortunately she did not heed the advice, she bought from another agent who would gladly take her cash.

Perhaps if we had a flat fee structure in our company all those years ago this lady would have believed us and valued the correct advice more than she ultimately did.

That's the potential value of a buying assistant to you.

How do you Find the Best Buying Assistant?

This part is easy. You email them and ask is it something they can do. Probably they will say no due to the fact that this is so uncommon in Spain.

For many agents, the possibility of earning 10,000 is better than the certainty of earning 3,000 euro or even 5,000 euro.

They must be willing to work for a flat fee and the good ones should also look for a percentage of money they save you on the purchase (I always liked to work on the basis of splitting all savings with the buyer – the more I saved them, the more I earned).

They must sign an agreement stating that they will charge you no commission but will work 35 or 40 hours on your behalf (if that much time is actually needed).

There can't be any additional fees for writing up contracts, etc.

They must do the majority of the work before you come here, writing and polishing your checklist, finding houses that match your criteria and in fact if they are on the ball they will know the house you are buying before you get on a flight here.

If you would like a free copy of the agreement which I used in our business for buying assistants, please email me. I'd be delighted to send it to you.

ian@iancomaskey.com

One time I did not sign an agreement with a buyer sticks in my mind.

One Saturday morning last September I was having breakfast with my little boy when a previous client of mine walked past. Lets call her Kathleen. We knew each other fairly well. I paid for her coffee.

She asked my advice on a few bits and pieces and she said that she wanted to buy something facing the sea. I told her my favorite development there. She was having difficulty with the Irish revenue and the potential purchase here had to be dealt with delicately she said.

Next day she came to see me – she wanted to buy one and was happy with the price of 180,000.

I knew her quite well so I offered a buying assistant service. I told her how I would secure her a saving of 13,000 euro.

She asked all the details and even involved her daughter and husband in what turned out to be a con job.

I had told her all the details, the selling agent, the short cuts and the commission. It was 10% but I was reducing my fee to a flat 5,000 euro.

What did Kathleen do? She went to the builder directly with exactly the system I had told her I would use to save her all that money. She managed through a web of lies from her and her daughter to get the full commission dropped off the price of the apartment.

She ripped me off - for 5,000!

Worse than all of that, as she is not supposed to have any assets outside of Ireland where she is declared bankrupt she opened the door to the Irish revenue finding out about her purchase in Spain. I don't understand the details of what she was trying to do with this part of the deal but something sounded really corrupt.

I console myself that although she ripped me off:

- *I know that my "buying assistant" system works – it works so well, she felt it was worth losing the friendship we had for her to get her hands on it.*

- *Now I always get the contracts signed first.*

- *Every single time Kathleen, her husband and her daughter put the key into the front door of their holiday home they will remember that she stole 5,000 euro to get it.*

- *When the revenue commissioners finally catch up with her, it will not have anything to do with me!*

Chapter review:

- *A buying assistant working on a flat fee basis is worth looking at for some clients.*

- *It's not for everyone.*

- *The more you intend to spend the more beneficial an assistant is.*

- *A buying assistant is not a salesperson.*

- *How Kathleen ripped me off and herself!*

Chapter Thirteen:
How do I Negotiate?

In this chapter:

- How do I negotiate?

- How do I negotiate even if I can't negotiate??

- Negotiation is not a sport- Its serious business.

- Donald Trump's 10,000 euro trick.

"The first thing to decide before you walk into any negotiation is what to do if the other fellow says no." ~ **Ernest Bevin**, *founder and General Secretary of the British General and Transport trade union, 1922-1940.*

So, you've got your buying assistant or at least a good estate agent in place.

You've gone through your checklist, viewed a few properties, and found one you really like. You and the estate agent are now buddies, teammates, working together on the same side. Now it's time to negotiate with the buyer.

But wait, doesn't the estate agent or the buying assistant do that?

Possibly. But it's just as important for you to know how to negotiate as well. Even if you never talk to the buyer, you still need to know what you want, what you're willing to give up, and how to make the deal.

Besides, the estate agent may not be as strong a negotiator as they are at showing properties, and even if they are, you're still the one making the decisions.

There are three possible outcomes from any negotiation:

- A deal is reached

- No deal is reached and the communication is over

- No deal is reached, but there is hope of a compromise and maybe a second round of talks

Obviously outcome 1 is the best and outcome 2 the worst, but don't discount outcome 3.

Outcome 3 is where you can make sure that everyone involved is happy, and nothing gets left on the table.

There are five steps to successful negotiation:

- **Know what you want.** Remember your checklist? Look back over it and figure out what you want the most, what you're willing to give up, particularly in the areas of price and timeframe. If the house is just perfect and you must have it, reexamine how much you'd be able to pay. If you have less money available now, consider being willing to pay a slightly higher price in return for a favourable payment plan. If the house is not in perfect shape, think about willingness to fix it up yourself vs. having the current owner do it.

- **Know what your next best option is**. What happens if this deal falls through? Knowing that the house around the corner is for sale too – maybe it's not perfect and needs a little TLC but the owner will accept a decent offer – is very different from thinking that it's either this house or nothing. Explore your options.

- **Know what the seller wants**. This is where negotiation can create magic. Ask the seller straight up what is important to them. It might not just be cash. Maybe the buyer wants to sell but not complete the deal for the next six months; maybe he needs a massive down payment today as he is on the verge of bankruptcy; maybe he only wants to see a nice family buy the house he has toiled all his life to build. Once you understand what the seller wants, you can work to give them exactly that —in return for what you want.

- **Know what the seller's next best option is**. This is something the agent can find out for you. If the seller can wait six months, that's different from a seller who needs to be home in Germany in 30 days. Are there other offers on the table? You've seen the house, do you think (or does your agent think) other clients might offer more for it than you? The seller will know their next best options the same way you know yours. Learning what they are will help inform your negotiations.

- **Know when to walk away**. If the seller simply refuses to give you the important things you want, or will only accept things you absolutely can't or don't want to give, it's okay to cut your losses and move on. Give the negotiation as much time as you feel comfortable giving it, but don't get fooled into beating a dead horse for days or weeks longer. The more time you waste on a bad deal, the more likely you are to miss good deals on your second or third choices.

Here are several additional notes to consider on the art of negotiation:

- Have options, really do. The person who comes out best in a negotiation is the person who has the best options and who can happily walk away.

- People say not to offer an upper and lower range of prices. For example never tell a seller that you'll pay between 200,000 to 250,000. There is another school of thought that says you must offer a range like this. I personally think you should not offer a range, just a specific number. Ranges are softer and easier than numbers, but they will have to be distilled to numbers eventually, and can unintentionally start the negotiation higher or lower than you'd like.

- Whoever speaks first, loses. Ask the seller to name their price first. In negotiation, responding is nearly always better than acting first.

- Only accept less than what you want if you are getting something else to balance it. Example: you are happy to pay 100,000 but you need to move in within 30 days. The family is not ready to go until two months. Right, you can accept that but you want to pay 98,000 euro instead of 100,000, or have the furniture thrown in, or include a car they'd be selling anyway. (This balancing act of trading what you want can actually be fun!)

- Be very careful of lines like *"Well, there is someone looking at it tomorrow"*, *"There is a lot of interest in it"*, *"You've only got until 1pm tomorrow"* and *"it'll be sold to someone else."* These kinds of statements push you for the quick sale, and you will rarely come out favourable by going along with them. The only time you need to move super-fast is when there is already another offer on the table. Any kind of pressure from the seller should be a red flag for you as a buyer.

Here's some more to consider:

When you do reach a deal everyone's happy with, do not second-guess yourself. Pull the trigger and buy the house.

Remember, This is not a game. The objective is not to beat the other guy, it's to buy the house. Don't get too smart.

If you are well below your budget, don't get caught up in dickering over a thousand or two. You already have a great deal; now buy the house.

You don't have to fall in love with your agent/seller - if she helps you get the deal that you want, that's all you need.

Be realistic. If a seller is looking for 500,000 and you offer him 250,000, you've just insulted him. Not only will he not take your offer, he probably won't feel inclined to give you much in negotiations once you do give him an offer he'd pay attention to. Offers up to 20% below listed price are usually high enough for the seller to take them seriously. Anything less than that is disrespectful.

Banks negotiate too. If you are buying a repossession, don't offer what the bank wants. If your agent doesn't understand this and says you can't make an offer, make one anyway.

When you shake hands on a deal, mean it. Be nice to everyone in the room - you never know who you are dealing with or who is ultimately making decisions.

Trying too hard to be cool, emotionless and removed from the outcome has the opposite effect making you look weak.

Know how to sweeten the deal for the seller/agent. Never buy at auction (unless you really know your stuff).

Don't show all your cards. What this means is: don't tell the seller the absolute most you're willing to pay, because that's what they'll charge you. Share everything about what's important to you, but keep your financial limits to yourself.

Never say you are the decision maker. Always use the third person close. "I need to check that with my agent/wife/husband/cat." This will give you time to consider, and to get rid of any emotion you may be dealing with. If there is a 3rd person, imaginary or real, even the best negotiator can't influence them. They are your buffer.

Okay, so that's all well and good if you are comfortable negotiating.

But what if you are not a negotiator?

Are you nervous when you talk about money? Do you break out in a cold sweat when your hard earned cash is on the line? Do you sweat bullets?

That's fine.

If that's the case, do not negotiate. No more than you should perform open-heart surgery. If you can't negotiate, don't, at least not in person.

You have two choices:

- Get someone else to negotiate for you. This could be your agent, your buyer's assistant, your spouse, a family member, a buffer; someone you trust who is comfortable negotiating.

- Negotiate by email. This is so safe and simple.

Here's how email negotiation can work: You've seen the house that ticks 80% of your boxes.

Problem is, you sweat like a hostage when you are in any type of negotiation and you hate talking about money.

Send your agent an email.

You can do this from the hotel room or anywhere, just do not agree to meet the agent. Absolutely do not meet the sellers, you will only give away your tells and cost yourself money. I guarantee it.

Be short and professional yet tease them with an offer to pay a deposit.

Hi Ian,

Its Mick here, thanks for showing us three houses yesterday, we have made a decision.

I will pay 100,000 euro plus costs for the property reference 1234. I am happy to pay the deposit today and will sign all paperwork before I fly back to Aarhus tomorrow morning.

Please reply, by mail. I'm not picking up calls this trip.

I am looking forward to a positive result,

Mick.

Over to them now.

One of two things will happen in response to this email.

Either:

- you get the deal

- you don't

If a) that's great. Congratulations. If b) that's ok too. You can try again in a second email:

Hi Ian,

Mick here again.

I spoke to my partner and we can afford to increase our offer to 105,000 euro for reference 1234.

We are now back in Aarhus. My 3,000 euro deposit is with my Spanish solicitor, and I will instruct her to make the transfer to you immediately on receiving word the offer has been accepted.

Once again, I look forward to a positive result.

Mick

Again, either this works or it doesn't, and then you can send a third email, etc. Feel free to keep this up as long as you are comfortable.

A few questions I personally always ask an agent in any country before I view a property:

- How many viewings has it had?

- How many offers?

- How many declined offers?

- Why are the owners selling?

- How long have they lived here?

- Are there any bonuses we can get? ("That car parked in the driveway, will it be thrown in?" It's worth asking, worse case they say no).

- Are there any title issues? They may be simple, but better for you and your lawyer to know now.

- Parking issues?

- How many owners are on the deeds? I've seen owners try to sell property with their dead uncle still on the deeds.

- Is this really an east facing terrace? (My compass says it's west facing, making breakfast sunshine a difficulty)!

- Why can't I get a mobile phone signal? (Loads of regions in Spain have little or no mobile phone coverage and no WIFI, especially inland. Bad if you are moving there to work in your virtual office)!

- Can I get TV, proper TV, that shows sports from my country?

- Is it ok for my builder to inspect it? (Don't waste your youth on inspections but a basic inspection of water boilers, electrical work, roofs etc. is worth doing). I personally value the opinion of our Irish builder ahead of any architect.

- Engineers' reports in Spain are useless as a general rule whereas getting a quote from a registered builder to fix something is a much better indicator of the condition of the property.

- Will I be able to resell this property?

- What are the local taxes and stamp duty? Again, they vary by region.

- What are the community fees? They can vary from 20 euro pm to 2,000 pm.

- What happens if the deal falls apart? Is my deposit safe?

- Will the seller sign a "sellers agreement" if we settle on a price?

- Why do you recommend this particular lawyer?

- Will the lawyer give me free stuff like a power of attorney/will/N.I.E. number?

- Do the dustbin men come out this far?

- What is the crime rate here?

- How much are the electricity and water charges? Can I see a few bills from the previous owners? **Note**: You can save thousands by switching suppliers for phones, TV, internet, power etc. Most owners don't bother!!

- Is it rentable while I'm not here?

- Does your agency rent property and if so, what's your charge. (Don't skimp on this – 15% is a good number for long term, higher for short term).

Having all of this in writing is a good insurance policy if something goes wrong.

One final note on negotiation: The 10,000-euro-in-pocket trick.

I first heard this years ago from Millionaire investor, and author of "We want you to be Rich," Donald Trump. Trump says you should always take 10,000 euro in cash, notes no bigger than 50s and put it in your front jeans pocket. This is not to show to anyone but for you to know it's there. It tells your subconscious that you have it and that "I'm worthy to be at this negotiation table".

10,000 euro in cash is a serious wedge of money but if you are spending 100,000 or 200,000 euro on a house, its not that huge.

The bigger the deal, the more intimidating the negotiation.

Try it, it gives you serious strength and tricks your brain into a calmer state. (Just don't forget it's there when out celebrating later that evening in the bar. You don't want to lose it)!

Chapter review:

- The importance of knowing how to negotiate.

- If you can't do it, that's ok. Be honest with yourself, if you can't do it, don't even try.

- Find a buffer to do it for you.

- Negotiate by email.

Chapter Fourteen:
Becoming a Buying Agent

In this chapter:

- The most underused trick in the business of buying Property in Spain- Become your own agent.

- Save thousands of euro in minutes of effort.

You're about to become your own Spanish Real Estate Agent. Congratulations!

Okay, not quite. You don't have a certification yet, and you haven't listed any properties yet, but if you've read this far, you actually know everything you need to know to be an estate agent or buyer's agent.

Many deals in Spain involve two or even three estate agents, including a buyer's agent and a seller's agent. If a deal is reached the commission is split between all these agents. Why don't you become your own buyer's agent? Not only will you get the best price available, but you'll also get half or a third of the commission once the deal's done.

Here's how you do it:

Send the following email to the estate agent for a property you're interested in:

Dear Ian

My name is Pat,

I am an estate agent based in Moscow.

We have a mutual client who is interested in purchasing a property which you have listed on your web site..

Or ...We have a mutual client who is looking to buy a property for 250,000 euro with a sea view, whatever. (In reality this client is your wife/husband/4 yr old daughter/other family member, but don't tell the agent that!)

I wish to know the best price in your opinion for which reference 1234 will be bought and what commission I would expect to receive if a sale is made from a client I bring to you.

Please let me know at your convenience and I will arrange my client's trip to view the property.

Best wishes,

Pat.

This salesperson will be quite excited to receive this email! Not only has it brought them a very hot lead (industry lingo for an interested customer), it has done so without them having to go out and prospect for it. Plus there's no mention of inspection trips, and no list of 500 houses they need to show.

With an email like this, you could have an estate agent working on your behalf to get a price reduction and a high commission on the house—both of which will directly benefit you.

(Incidentally, this trick can work with any business that pays commission in exchange for leads—lawyers, mortgage brokers, TV installation companies, and many more).

Best case scenario: they not only email you the bottom line price on this house but a couple of alternatives too.

Check your list, ask for a few very specific options no higher than your price range and bingo – you soon know what's really available to you. And if the agent comes back with "sorry, we're not interested," you have lost nothing but the time it took you to write an email.

When the agent finds out you are representing yourself… will they really care?

Probably not. You did what you said you'd do, you brought a buyer to them, and got them a commission they wouldn't have gotten otherwise.

This might even become a dramatic career change for you. What if you not only pulled this off for yourself but did it for a few other people you know? Just like that, you're a buyer's assistant. Feel free to reach out to me if you'd like to try it, I'll help you compose some emails.

Chapter review:

- You can become an agent even if its just for your own deal or deals.

- Why not get paid a commission to buy your own house?

Chapter Fifteen:
Conclusion

In this chapter:

- One last true story from La Zenia in 1998.

As we wrap up, I'd like to share one last story with you. As you read it, ask yourself: with all the new Spanish real estate knowledge you've just learned, what would you do in this situation?

It's 1998 and the Spanish Property boom is just about to take off.

An Irish buyer came to La Zenia, Orihuela Costa and thought that it badly needed an Irish pub. There was no bar in the area despite the plane loads of property buyers and tourists landing in Alicante airport every week.

He approached the local estate agent, a Spanish guy who appeared to be trustworthy. Many buyers were already dealing with this guy. He had one unit left in the commercial centre Zenia Golf, La Zenia.

The price was a hefty one but the client negotiated the bottom line to 82,000 Irish pounds. They shook hands and agreed to meet next day in the agent's office around the corner from the unit to sign contracts, pay the deposit, etc.

The client showed up and upon reading the contract saw that the agent had somehow added on an additional 1,000 pounds, separate to fees, tax and commissions. The agent was pulling a fast one! The buyer explained the error and yet the agent told him that there was no mistake, the buyer was wrong and anyway, there was another client waiting for the unit. (Probably true in this case).

The buyer excused himself and went for a walk around the block. He knew he was being treated unfairly. No money had changed hands and walking away was the easiest thing he could have done. He made a decision that went against what every property-buying guide will tell you. He went back to the office, told the guy with a smile that the price was indeed the higher one, shook hands and completed the deal.

Would you have done the same thing?

Maybe not. But the buyer, Bernie Comaskey, went on to make seven figures in profits from Paddy's Point Irish bar over the next ten years. He eventually sold the bar for eight times what he paid for it.

Is there a right way to deal with someone you know is taking more than 1,000 euro straight from your pocket? Not really, but it feels pretty good when you can take that situation and turn it to your advantage anyway.

The point is, things do not always go the way you want them to. Sellers will take furniture they should leave, tax will be higher than you thought, the agent will not be available when she said she would, the lawyer is never in when you need him, it might even rain one day.

Play the cards you've been dealt, trust your gut, and you'll make the right decisions for you too.

So there you have it.

This is the absolute 100% guaranteed way to save on time, stress and cash when you are buying a property in Spain. This system works all the time, for any buyer who chooses to use it.

Good luck and please share your success stories with us.

Buena Suerte, mi amigo!

Thank You!

Thank you for downloading this book. I really, really appreciate it and I hope you get something from it. The most rewarding thing you could now do for me is to review the book on Amazon (positive and negative feedback is welcome).

Please tell me what you think and even negative feedback will help me get it right next time.

Don't forget to download your free audio book.

Thank you very much,

Ian Comaskey

Further Reading Material

Robert Kiyosaki: Rich Dad Poor Dad: What the Rich Teach their Kids about Money that the Poor and Middle-Class Do Not

Robert G. Allen: Multiple Streams of Income

Richard Koch: The 80/20 Principle

Donald Trump: Think Like A Billionaire: Everything You Need to Know About Success, Real Estate, and Life

Brian Tracy: The Psychology of Achievement

Tim Ferriss: The 4 Hour Work Week

About the Author

Ian Comaskey is a business person, property investor, occasional writer and these days *very occasional* estate agent.

Ian has been selling property in Spain since 2002 having established the successful real estate company, Comaskey Properties that year, later to be joined by his uncle Fehin. Comaskey Properties has three office locations on the Orihuela Costa, and has grown to incorporate a property management division and a long term rental department while simultaneously securing over 2,000 purchases for its clients. Total sales in Spain for Comaskey Properties to date are in excess of 200 million euro.

Ian's diverse business interests over the years include buying and selling property, renting commercial property in Spain and in Ireland, hairdressers, cafes and bars, a wine shop, internet cafe, personalised jigsaws and recently becoming a partner in a corporate gifts firm.

Ian first became interested in the mistakes people make when buying property during the years of soaring property prices in Spain when he observed that more than 60% of buyers bought something different to what they actually wanted to buy, often with disastrous financial consequences.

The Comaskey family—Ian, his wife Lynne, and children Finn and Ruari - currently live in La Zenia, Orihuela Costa, Spain.

Appendix

Please note.

All information provided here has been done with the kind permission of Spanish Solutions Legal and Tax firm.

Information is correct at the time of going to print October 2014.

Please refer directly to Spanish Solutions for more detailed information.

www.spanishsolutions.net

What are the general costs involved with buying a property in Spain?

The costs of buying a house depend on whether the house is a new build property, or a re-sale. In all cases, on top of the purchase price, you will need to pay the Notary Fees and Registration. Then taxes are due dependent on the house type, as detailed.

• **NOTARY FEES**

This is the charge that the Notary will make for the Purchasing/Selling process and paperwork. This covers the printing and amending of the Escritura (Title Deeds) and the Notary witnessing the signing of it.

• **REGISTRATION**

The Land Registry will make a charge for the registering of the change of ownership details of the property.

• **IMPUESTO DE TRANSMISIONES: Re-Sale Properties**

This is calculated at 10% of the value of the house as stated on the Escritura (Title Deeds), for Re-Sale Properties only.

• **IVA: New Build Properties**

IVA is paid directly to the builder, either in stages with the payments, or at the final payment and is presently at rate of 10%.

ACTOS JURIDICOS DOCUMENTADOS 1,5% of the Title Deeds price, which must be paid to the local Administration within 30 days following the signing at the Notary.

Spanish Solutions can provide impartial representation and translation for Notary processes and assistance with all elements of purchasing a property. If you would like any help, please contact them on 00 34 966761741 or sales@spanishsolutions.net

Buying or Selling a property in Spain? Does it have a Habitation Certificate?

If you are intending to sell your property in Spain you must have a current Habitation certificate "Cedula de Habitabilidad".

These are issued by the town hall to a builder on completion of new properties, stating each property has been passed as habitable. Once obtained, the Habitation Certificate has a validity of five years and states that the building conforms to the original plans submitted to the town hall.

When the five years expires, the owner of the property should renew the certificate via the town hall, who will issue the new certificate, a Licencia de Segunda Ocupación in the name of the owner of the property.

If any refurbishments are made to the property (including the closing in of patio areas, paving of gardens, adding of additional rooms etc.) permission should be obtained from the town hall prior to starting the works.

The representatives of any buyers will now ask for a certificate that is in date, and many clients are finding that they need to get this renewed before selling their property. Unfortunately, this is also when the Town Hall will become aware of any minor works made without permission.

If you are planning to sell your house, you should get help from us at Spanish Solutions to organise your paperwork so as to avoid delays – let's face it, it's hard enough to find buyers for properties at the moment, and what you don't want is to lose a buyer. If you are buying a property, check the situation regarding the Habitation Certificate and take advice from us or you could possibly have a problem.

Spanish Solutions offers a range of services including the obtaining of this certificate and gaining of planning permissions. If you would like any help, please contact them on 00 34 966761741 or sales@spanishsolutions.net.

Do you need a Spanish Will?

A person with either UK or Irish resident nationality who has assets in Spain, in the form of property, bank accounts etc. should make a Will detailing exactly what they wish to happen in the event of death. Whenever there is more than one person listed on the title deeds of a property, a Will should be made by each person.

Under Art 9 of the Spanish Civil Code, a foreign national is entitled to leave assets according to the national law of their country of origin, so when a foreigner dies with property in Spain, their <u>nationality</u> usually dictates the law that applies to the distribution of their assets.

The proceedings will take place in Spain, however, following the Spanish process, and can be lengthy. If there is no Spanish Will and you die in Spain, the death certificate will need to be obtained at the local Civil Registry. If in Ireland or the United Kingdom, an original death certificate would need to be obtained from the General Register Office in the home country. This certificate, any Grant of Probate and a foreign Will need to be officially translated into Spanish, apostilled and presented in Spain.

If you are living in Spain and a resident, a Spanish Will is likely to apply only to your assets in Spain and would have no legality in any other country, if you have become a Spanish citizen, matters may be different and it would be wise to take legal advice. You would still need a separate Will in a country where you have assets still.

What would happen regarding inheritance tax in Spain?

Unlike some countries, there is no exemption from inheritance tax between husband and wife. A tax form must be completed and the taxes paid. In Spain it is the heir who is taxed and not the estate. Tax will be calculated on the relationship of the heir to the deceased and the value of the inheritance he/she receives.

The inheritance tax must be paid within six months of the death of the deceased; a request for further six months' extension may be filed although interest will be charged. Executors are not normal in Spain. Legal title passes directly to the beneficiaries.

Spanish Solutions offers a range of services including assistance making a Will or with an Inheritance process. Tel: 00 34 966761741 or sales@spanishsolutions.net

Renting Out your Spanish Property

As many property owners are considering renting out their property in Spain in order to generate a little income to cover their ownership expenses and pay for their trips to Spain etc., we thought we should draw your attention towards the main points that you should remember in relation to this:

- In Spain the law in very based towards the tenant. The law that relates to renting out property is "La Ley de Arrendamiento Urbanos" - 29/1994, November 24th

- It is recommended to have a rental contract with the identity of the landlord and the tenants, the address of the property, the duration of the rental property, and the amount of the rent

- A deposit should be taken, equal to one month's rent and refundable at the end of the contract

- With regard to the duration of the contract - this can be mutually agreed between both parties but Spanish law dictates that after one year has passed, annual renewal of the contract is obligatory up to a minimum of 5 years.

- For this reason many contracts are usually for 11 months initially. The contract can then only be cancelled in the event that the tenant gives 30 days prior notice of cancellation or that the landlord requires the return of the property for his own use as a permanent home

- If the contract is 5 years or more, then if neither party gives 30 days prior notice of cancellation the contract can be extended a further year up to a maximum of 3 years.

- Payment of utilities and council tax and community fees are generally decided at the outset, and agreed between both parties and included in the contract.

- Repairs and Building Works:

According to the law, the landlord is responsible for any necessary repairs to the property to keep it habitable but not if the damage is caused by the tenant. In turn the tenant is responsible for informing the landlord of any damage. If the damage is serious and needs urgent repair then the tenant can undertake this, then request payment from the landlord.

Small day to day repairs are the responsibility of the tenant and as the law does not stipulate what a small repair is, it is advisable to stipulate a maximum cost in the contract.

Building works to modify the property must be authorised by the landlord. It is sensible to attach an inventory of furniture and fittings to the contract.

If you are considering renting out your property you should be aware that depending on whether you are non resident or resident in Spain, income derived from renting is taxed differently. If you have any queries regarding your tax affairs contact info@spanishsolutions.net.

Spanish Solutions regularly prepare rental contacts (in Spanish and English).

They are also able to introduce you to local property agents who deal with long term rentals of properties or sale of properties should you wish to discuss this with someone.

Buying or setting up a business on the Costa Blanca.

Buying a business in Spain can be a very exciting and challenging prospect, as well as being a big step, it can be very time consuming so make sure you have all of the information you need.

As a foreigner you really needs to be aimed at other foreigners or holidaymakers, the Spanish do not usually patronize foreign businesses unless they are offering something unique. However with the large increase in residential tourism taking place at present there are new opportunities springing up all the time.

Don't get taken for a ride

There are many examples of being duped. In Spain if you are not buying the freehold of the premises then you will be paying for the "Trespaso". This is for the goodwill, internal fittings, plant and stock of the business. You will then rent the premises from a landlord, who will require a deposit. These are all critical areas where problems can arise.

Opening Licence. See it and get a copy. This should be available at the premises. If the actual licence or a copy cannot be provided then the business does not exist legally. You can agree to buy the business without the licence and negotiate the price accordingly, but get quotes on the costs and likelihood of eventually obtaining a license first.

The final costs of meeting the various criteria and obtaining an opening licence ('Apertura' in Spanish) for a particular business is a large variable. If a business you are considering buying has applied for a licence, and is running pending acceptance of the application, then ascertain exactly (from the authorities, not the seller) why it is delayed and what the current status of the application is.

We always recommend that you leave a small contingency to cover issues such as opening licences, reforms and updates etc. In most cases, for example, in respect of an opening licence - a simple change of name is required if there is a proper licence in place.

On a regional level, certain business activities are required to obtain activity-specific licenses, such as travel agencies, tattoo parlours, auto body repair shops, etc. Some licenses you will have to pay a fee for.

Depending on what your proposed business is, other types of licenses may be required as well. When a change of name happens, regulations may have changed that you need a disabled toilet or more fire extinguishers for example. Your business accountant can check all this for you. We are experienced in this area.

Not a license per se, you should also be prepared to charge Value Added Tax on goods and services (*Impuesto sobre el Valor Añadido, IVA*), which ranges from 4-21%. The tax rules are governed by different plans depending on what your business is. Check with your tax adviser regarding your tax and reporting obligations.

Your business will also need a "Visitors Book" (*Libro de Visita*). You must acquire it from your province's *Dirección Provincial del Ministerio de Trabajo y Asuntos Sociales* and have it available at all times for labour and Social Security inspectors.

Rental contract. You must get a copy of this. It will show;

(a) How much longer it has to run

(b) Who is responsible for what type of wear and tear

(c) What percentage of the trespaso relates to the landlord, what fittings belong to whom

(d) If the seller has the right to sell the lease

(e) Whether it is renewable at the end of its term

(f) when and what any rent increases might be

(g) Whether you can sell the business on again

(h) Who pays for what-refuse collection, electricity, water, rates, taxes etc.

(i) All the other terms a tenant is required to comply with.

Trespaso. Don't pay too much. If you pay more than its worth (fittings, etc) a lot of your capital will have been consumed immediately. Goodwill is intangible, so be sensible about this.

Landlord. It is a legal requirement that you contact this person when the tenancy is changing hands. Paying too much rent is probably the biggest single cause of business failure in Spain so make sure you agree with the landlord the exact rent required and any contract changes.

Contract of sale. Get a copy beforehand-you must read and understand everything in the contract, so that you can check everything carefully well before the day of signing. The contract should specify every item which is included in the sale, the terms and timescales involved and guarantee that the business is free of encumbrance, debts and liabilities.

Notarial approval. If you don't "Notarise" the signing of the contract and handing over of the money your ownership may be challenged at a later date and you may not be able to claim tax allowances against your capital outlay.

Type of tax status. You will need to discuss this with a tax adviser. Being self-employed is generally less expensive than having a limited company, especially as they can have all sorts of hidden liabilities and a thorough check must be carried out on them by a professional.

Also bear in mind;

(a) Taxes are higher than a "sole proprietor"

(b) Costs of formation are comparatively high.

(c) Annual audited accounts are necessary and the appointment of an "administrator" is mandatory to comply with all the statutory obligations of a limited company.

VAT

Legalities

Most documents in our modern, complex world are necessary to prove that you;

(a) Are legally identifiable and entitled to be where you are doing what you are doing.

(b) Can produce the documents necessary to prove you are the real owner of anything you claim to own.

(c) Have met every statutory requirement relating to either of the above.

Make sure you can produce any necessary documents, e.g., residencia, trade licence, statutory payment receipts (social security, rates, license fees) when required to do so.

Professionals

Don't use a lawyer to fight a case, use him to avoid a case by consulting him before problems arise. Ensure that any documentation associated with your business (from the rental contract through to your terms of business with your clients) has been correctly worded and is legally effective in protecting your interests. A good accounting service will always save you money, more so in Spain than in other places.

Capital

Don't overstretch yourself. Remember that higher than normal start up costs and lower turnover will call for some funds in reserve.

Good Service

Whether you are beginning an enterprise you have no previous experience in, or continuing your own profession, you must do it well. Do not start something beyond your capabilities.

Once you've successfully chosen a name and a legal structure for your business, created a business plan, found financing and a location, and secured licenses and permits, then you can start to hire employees (this also requires advice from a professional), create a website, advertise and perform all the other tasks that will contribute to the success of your very own Spanish business.

Costs of Buying and Owning a Property In Spain

When buying property in Spain, always keep digital and hard copies of all invoices related to your purchase. Likewise, if you ever do building work on the property once you own it, keep copies of all licences and invoices. You may be able to offset these expenses against capital gains when you sell, and so reduce your Capital gains tax on a sale.

It is important to have clear from the outset the real costs you will face when you buy property in Spain. It is equally important to be clear about the ongoing costs you will face as a property owner in Spain.

It is your responsibility to be informed and do your own numbers, rather than rely on the claims of others. Here we explain all the different types of costs, but bear in mind that the actual cost will depend on your particular circumstances.

As a buyer of a property in Spain there are a number of costs and taxes over and above the property price that you will have to pay. Depending upon whether you are buying a new property from a developer, or a resale property from a private individual, you will either have to pay VAT & Stamp Duty, or a transfer tax. The different cases are explained below, along with the other costs and taxes that are common to both cases.

New Build From a Developer or Bank

VAT & Stamp Duty (**IVA & AJD**)

These taxes apply for residential properties being sold for the first time (never previously occupied), or for commercial properties and plots of land. This is a national tax, so VAT is the same wherever the property is located.

At present VAT (known as IVA in Spain) is 10% on the purchase price of residential properties (villa, apartment, etc), and 21% for commercial properties and plots of land.

The Stamp duty (known as AJD) is 1.5% of the price of the purchase, but might go up in some regions, so be sure to check on the latest rate. Both VAT and Stamp Duty are paid by the buyer.

Resale

Transfer Tax (**ITP**)

This tax applies if the property is deemed to be a second transfer (i.e. a re-sale, not the first time a newly built home is bought), and is paid by the buyer. The general (national) rule of ITP is 10%. Income Tax Provision When Buying From Non-residents If the seller is not a Spanish resident, the buyer has to withhold 3% of the purchase price and pay it to the tax authorities (application form 211). If this is not done the property will be considered by the tax authorities as the asset backing the capital gains tax liability of the seller. This condition is very unlikely to apply when purchasing from a developer.

Costs that affect both new build and resale property purchases

Agency Fees

Estate agency fees or commissions are paid by the seller, unless otherwise agreed. If the buyer uses a search agency then search fees are paid by the buyer.

Agents charge between 2% and 15% of the sale price, depending upon the region and type of property. Unless the buyer has specifically agreed to pay the agent's fee this cost will be built into the sale price.

Legal Fees

You are strongly advised to hire a lawyer to help you during the buying process. Your lawyer drafts and reviews contracts on your behalf and can explain all the legal and administrative issues you face. Your lawyer should also carry out any necessary due diligence (checking ownership claim of the seller, charges on the property, permits, etc.) and arrange all the required documents to complete the process (property registration, tax payments, etc.).

Legal fees for a purchase without any complications and charged for the process should be in the region of 1,000 to 2,500 Euros.

Mortgage costs

If you choose to buy with a mortgage then this will incur several additional costs. First there will be the property valuation that the mortgage provider will require before granting the mortgage. Then there will be the costs of the mortgage itself. This varies according to the provider, and even according to the particular branch. However there is usually some kind of opening fee of around 1% of the value of the mortgage. Finally a mortgage will increase the Notary expenses.

Notary Expenses

Notary expenses are nearly always paid by the buyer and are calculated in relation to the purchase price declared in the deeds of sale. To be on the safe side you should calculate Notary fees as being 1% of the purchase price declared in the deeds of sale. In many cases however Notary fees are more like 0.5% (or less) of the price declared in the deeds.

Property Registry Inscription Fees

Expenses related to inscribing the sale with the land registry are also nearly always paid by the buyer, and are calculated in relation to the purchase price declared in the deeds of sale. To be on the safe side you should calculate 1% of the purchase price declared in the deeds, though once again it depends upon the property and the area, and the fee could be considerably lower.

<u>In Summary, allow for up to 15% of the purchase price in taxes and other costs</u>.

If the buyer takes out a mortgage these costs can be somewhat higher due to an additional public deed for the mortgage and the inevitable bank charges involved. In this case transaction costs might reach between 10% and 12% of the value of the property purchased.

Banking Costs

To pay for the property, you will more than likely need to write a banker's cheque. In order to do that, you will need to open an account in a Spanish bank and transfer money from the bank in your country. The cost of transferring the money can go up to 0,4% of the amount transferred. The banker's cheque will most likely cost 0,5% of its amount.

Furniture Costs

Once you own a property you will need to furnish it. The cost of furnishing a property depends entirely upon what you want. Of course there is no limit to how much you can spend, though you can also get away with it on a tight budget (all from IKEA, for example).

Costs of Owning the Property

There will of course be costs associated with owning a property in Spain. Some of these will be maintenance costs, such as cleaning, repairing, reforming, utility bills, rubbish collection, and so on. These will be determined by the size and type of the property you buy. Obviously a large villa with a garden and pool will require much more effort and cost to maintain than a small apartment. For cleaning a figure of 10 Euros an hour is fairly typical throughout Spain.

Apart from the general maintenance costs referred to above, there are a number of costs in the form of taxes and fees that property owners in Spain face.

Property Ownership Tax (IBI)

A local tax on the ownership of property in Spain, irrespective of whether the owner is a resident or not. Calculated on the basis of the valor catastral (an administrative value that is usually lower than the market value, sometimes considerably so) set by the town hall the tax rate goes from 0.4% – 1.1% of the valor catastral depending on the Spanish region.

Personal Income Tax (IRNR)

Non-residents who own property in Spain have to pay an annual income tax that varies according to whether the property is rented out or not.

Not rented out Non-resident property owners who do not rent out their property and who do not have any other source of income in Spain pay income tax based on the value of their property.

Rented out If non-residents rent out their property and receive an income in exchange, they are obliged by law to declare this income and pay taxes on it. The taxable base and the tax rate will be determined by the laws as they apply to each person's particular circumstances (taking into account the double taxation treaty – if any – between Spain and the country of origin of the non-resident). In many cases non-residents simply pay a flat rate of 25% of the gross income they earn from their property in Spain.

Residents in Spain will have to pay the income tax based on their income earned during the year. The tax rate depends on the level of income.

Community Fees

Owners of property that is part of any development, building, or complex in which common zones are shared with other owners are by law obliged to be members of the community of owners, know as the Comunidad de Propietarios. This will entail paying community fees for the upkeep of the common areas, and any other services that the community vote for. The fees will vary according to the magnitude of the common areas, the costs of maintaining them, and the services that the community vote for. A budget for annual community expenses is approved by majority vote of all owners (or representatives) who are present at the annual general meeting of the Comunidad de Propietarios.

Insurance

Household insurance will vary according to the circumstances of the owner and the type of property. However it should be born in mind as a cost that all property owners will face.

MOVING TO SPAIN CHECK LIST

If you are looking to enjoy a permanent or non-permanent life in Spain, we recommend you follow this advice below:-

Advice before buying a property:

- Find a lawyer who speaks good English as well as Spanish, who will explain everything properly to you and detail the costs. They will carry out searches, as it is vital to check a property is free of debts, has a title deed, check licences, make sure all documents are in order and ensure the property has been built properly (or even been built!) and legally without claims on it from a third party

- Apply for a NIE number (identification number for foreigners). You will need it to buy a property, car, setting up a bank account, get a new mobile phone etc.

- Make sure you are aware of the taxes and costs you will incur; 10% buying tax, notary and land registry fees, legal fees, any mortgage costs, wills, NIES, house insurance, and power of attorney, if needed.

- It is important that you have a First Occupation Licence for your house if you are buying from a builder. You can buy it without the First Occupation Licence but you need to be aware that then you may have to pay the Town Hall and architect for a new one. So it is not illegal to sell a property without an LFO, but it is illegal to force a buyer to complete without one. The developer is contractually obliged to produce an LFO at the time of completion and not doing so would be breach of contract (unless the buyer waives this obligation).

- In the Valencia Region (including the Orihuela Costa), if you are buying a resale property it should have a Licence of Second Occupation. The original LFO is for 5 years. After 5 years, if there is going to be a change of ownership, the seller needs to apply for a Licence of Second Occupation. It is the seller's responsibility.

- If moving funds and changing currency, seek specialist advice on transferring your money to Spain without high bank charges and poor exchange rates.

Once a property is purchased:-

- Register at the local Town Hall on the "Padron". This is the equivalent of placing yourself on the voters roll in Spain. The Padron enables the town hall to do a head count on the number of permanent dwellers in the area and therefore petition for grants to maintain and improve the infrastructure. The Padron Certificate is needed to register at a health centre, getting children into school and also for a variety of other matters. It has a validity between 30 – 90 days, however once obtained only needs to be updated when you actually need to show it to the authorities.

- Apply for a Residencia. All EU citizens planning to reside in Spain for more than three months per year must obtain the form of Residents Certificate (**Residencia**). This is the green Certificate issued by the offices of Extranjeria/National Police.

- The Residents certificate is a document that certifies your residence in Spain with the Central Register of Foreigners (*Registro Central de Extranjeros*) and lists your name, where you live, your nationality, the date you registered, and your Foreigner's Identity Number (the **NIE**). Having a Residents Certificate does not mean that you are fiscally resident. A fiscal resident means you file income tax returns in Spain. Your NIE and Residencia can be in one document.

- If your country has a reciprocal agreement with Spain, apply for a S1 form to obtain a medical card. If not covered by the Social Security system, it is essential to take out a private medical plan.

- If your car has a foreign registration plate, sell it, or change the registration to Spanish plates.

- Exchange your driving licence for a Spanish one.

- Pay your local urbanisation community fees, if there are any.

- Pay every year the Town Hall taxes (IBI/Suma, which is like local rates, car road tax)

- Pay annually either the income tax declaration, or if only in Spain less then 183 days per year, the non-resident tax declaration.

- Those who have assets in Spain, especially property, should write a Spanish Will to avoid delays and complications when they die.

- If you are considering improvements to your house, either small or large works, inside or outside, you must apply for a building licence from the local town hall.

- If you are planning to work on a self-employed basis you need to talk to an adviser about how to do this legally, and if you have premises about the correct licences.

Going to live in Spain? Do you need to become a Resident?

From 28 March 2007, Royal Decree 240/07 required that all EU citizens planning to reside in Spain for **more than 3 months** must obtain the new form of **Residencia** to show their **residency**. This is the **Residencia green Certificate** issued by various offices of Extranjeria/National Police.

The A4 printed Residence Certificate states your name, address, nationality, NIE number (*Número de Identificación Extranjeros*) and date of registration. The new **Residencia Certificate** is for life – it never expires.

We should make clear that this is not a fiscal Residency Certificate which is a certificate you need when registering with the Spanish tax authorities.

A Residencia Certificate is a certificate that you are registered officially as a foreigner living in Spain, but not for tax purposes. To get this you need 2 photos, Padron (dated within 3 months), deeds or rental contract, original passport, and "Vidal Laboral", a sort of history of working life in Spain, from the nearest social security office, or if not working evidence of private medical insurance and income details (from the paying companies) and the S1 form from the DHSS in the UK or equivalent in other countries.

Also, it is obligatory for anyone staying in Spain for more than six months to obtain a **Padron**. This is the equivalent of placing yourself on the voters roll in Spain. The Padron enables the town hall to do a head count on the number of permanent dwellers in the area and therefore petition for grants to maintain and improve the infrastructure.

The Padron Certificate is needed to register at a health centre and also for a variety of other institutions including getting children into school and a car registered. The Padron has a validity between 30 – 90 days, however only needs to be updated when you actually need to show it to the authorities.

Spanish Solutions offers a range of services including obtaining the NIE, Residencia and Padron certificates. If you would like any help, please contact them on sales@spanishsolutions.net or 0034 966760917 or 966761741.

Printed in Great Britain
by Amazon